Girl, God's Not Done

Simple Steps To Loving You Like God Does

Dr. Catherine Goodall Jackson

This book offers a resource to discover how your identity as a beloved child of God fuels your self-worth and empowers you to love yourself authentically

iiiii! I am SUPER EXCITED that you took the time to pick up this book!

This has been four… maybe five years in the making. The book was finished, edited, and even accepted by publishers—and still, I wasn't happy. I didn't feel like it was exactly what God required of me. LOL… OK, let's be real: writing a book about loving yourself the way God intends, while not fully embracing what you're saying, is pretty hypocritical.

I felt like an absolute imposter! I also felt like the book had evolved into something that no longer represented me or how I communicate.

A phenomenal publisher took a 70-page version of me "talking on paper" and turned it into a nearly 300-page novel that even impressed me! But let's just say… I was googling too many words (covering my face).

I tried for months (maybe years) to edit it into something I could relate to, but that became a daunting task. So the book sat… for a couple more years.

Then I started listening to Yvonne Orji's Bamboozled by Jesus, and right at the beginning, she said:

"Someone you've never met is counting on you. They're waiting on your 'yes'—to live your dreams out loud so that they, too, can dream new dreams and believe in more than their circumstances dictate." That was the push I needed to get back to it.

Now that I've rambled, let me take a moment to introduce myself. I am Dr. Catherine Jackson. I have a BA in Sociology, an MBA, and a PhD in Pastoral Psychology. I'm a certified John Maxwell Coach and Trainer, as well as an international speaker and event host. I'm DISC certified. I spent about 12 years as a marketing executive for some of the largest fast-moving consumer goods companies in the Caribbean and Latin America. I also served as Director of Project Development for one of the region's largest non-profits. For over 20 years, I've worked on some of the biggest entertainment productions in Jamaica, South Florida, and New York. I've worked for an NBA player, lived in Jamaica, South Florida, New York City, and Colorado, and traveled to every continent—visiting places like Vanuatu and Essaouira.

I share all this because I have so much to be grateful for when I look back at my life.

BUT the journey has been ROUGH!

I've made some really poor decisions in my life—but God!
God has managed to turn all my bad choices into something spectacular.

He showed a very insecure girl some grace and opened my eyes to the truth: I didn't know who I was. I didn't understand who He created me to be. I didn't love myself or see myself through His eyes.

God took me on a journey to fall in love with the person He created—and I believe He's called me to share those Simple Steps with you.

If you're not a Jesus lover, it doesn't matter in this moment. I truly believe the Bible is a guide to life, and just like any book, there's something to learn.

Rabbi Saul Rubin said—and I've come to accept:

"We have stories to tell, stories that provide wisdom about the journey of life. What more have we to give one another than our 'truth' about our being human, and share our adventure as honestly and as openly as we know how?"

I wasn't a typical girl growing up. There was no "princessification" of me. I didn't wear dresses, didn't like dolls, and loved climbing and running around.

I had pixie-short hair until 9th grade, and people often mistook me for a boy. I went to an all-girls Catholic high school, and I was always chosen to play the male role in any production.

Needless to say, when I started growing my hair in 9th grade, that awkward, shapeless afro phase was not flattering.

I was friends with all the pretty and popular girls in elementary, prep, and high school—but I was too insecure to feel like I could be one of them. I chose instead to be one of the boys and reveled in my realm of "tomboydom."

In college, I fell into a pattern of dating one uncaring and unfaithful boy after another—but that's a story for later. I didn't know my value. The same was true for some "friendships." I didn't protect myself. I didn't value myself. And as a result, I was treated accordingly. It always felt like I was trying to fit into a mold someone else had designed for me. I became quite the chameleon. I prioritized everyone else's needs over my own—even when it wore me down physically, emotionally, and spiritually. Because I lacked boundaries, I allowed myself to be taken advantage of and taken for granted.

Anyway—this is not a pity party! This is me sharing how I was able to overcome so many things I hope you never have to go through just to become who God has called you to be.

I'll be taking you through some Simple Steps to love yourself more: More than your poor choices. More than the people who took you for granted. More than you've loved yourself in the past.

I'm looking forward to taking this journey with you. I pray it's a fruitful one.

"You cannot truly love another until you know how to love yourself. You cannot love yourself or another until you fill up with and express God's love. You cannot pour from an empty cup." - Anonymous

STEP 1: Keep it SIMPLE

"If you begin where God began, you will end up where God wants you to end up."

Pastor Christopher Morgan, DNA

What grounds you?
What do you value?

I was always raised to have manners, to treat everyone with respect, and to treat others the way I wanted to be treated. I was taught not to tell lies because there was NOTHING my mother hated more than a liar! She would always say, "A liar always turns into a thief," which leads to... I was taught to be kind. I had a good work ethic, and I always tried to give my best in anything I did (outside of schoolwork).

The questions I asked you at the beginning... What grounds you? What do you value? I had to ask myself those questions.

For too long, I was busy pleasing everyone. I became a chameleon—whoever I needed to be to fit in with whatever group I was in or situation I was facing. I didn't know who I was. "No" was not in my vocabulary. I was in an abusive relationship for about six years, and before that, I was just moving wherever the wind blew me—with no real sense of direction or purpose. The only time I remember having "goals" was in 9th grade when I vocalized wanting to be a flight attendant so I could travel the world. My father was a pilot, and many of my "aunties" were flight attendants or worked at Air Jamaica. I also wanted to be married by 27 and have four children. My mother was married by 27 and has four children. LOL

There are a couple of things I did know: I knew I always had to feel like I was in "control," which meant no drinking, smoking, or taking drugs of any kind. I was the designated driver. I was the one who showed up for everyone. I was the caregiver—to a fault—even if it meant I was losing or sacrificing. Some may say I had a savior complex—that compulsion to help others even when they don't need or want it.

In case you were wondering if you have it, here are some signs:
- You feel responsible for helping others
- You feel like you need to fix everybody's problems
- You volunteer, donate, or advocate for causes
- You continue to help even when it's not helpful or harmful
- You insist on helping others, even if they don't want it
- You neglect your own needs

These all sound like good things, but they can lead to very unhealthy dynamics in relationships and will eventually cause personal distress.

If you only feel good about yourself when you're helping someone… or you believe helping others is your purpose… or you spend so much energy trying to help others that you neglect yourself—it's a problem. This is what happened to me.

I had to take several steps back and think about what actually matters to me.

Who am I? Who do I want to be… What do I need to do to become that person? Then I realized, what I REALLY needed to understand was: Who was I created to be?

10

My relationship with God was lukewarm, I would say. I knew Him. We were cool. Church was a thing for me. I would go to the club or a party on Saturday and be at church Sunday morning serving as an usher. In college, I would go to church on Saturday night and then head to the club.

Fast forward to post-college—well, post-first attempt at college (we'll talk more about that later)—God and I got a LOT closer, and He started to hold me accountable in ways I was not prepared for. God took me to the beginning…

> *"So God created mankind in His own image, in the image of God He created them; male and female He created them." —***Genesis 1:27**

Wait, what?! I was created in the image of God? There's more…

"And God blessed them, and God said to them, 'Be fruitful and multiply, and fill the earth and subdue it, and have dominion over the fish of the sea and over the birds of the heavens and over every living thing that moves on the earth.'"

So, God created ME in HIS image AND He wants me to be fruitful, multiply, and have DOMINION?!

C.S. Lewis says, "We are what we believe we are."

I believed that God made me. I also believed that He made me in His image because He said it. I was fruitful—I multiplied—because I poured so much into others, and their lives were better. (This is me rationalizing.)

But what does He mean when He says I am to have DOMINION? I had to flesh that out some more.

Who am I – I am a child of THE KING.

What grounds me – His Word… OK – what else?

"Love the Lord your God with all your heart and with all your soul and with all your mind and with all your strength. 'The second is this: 'Love your neighbor as yourself.' There is no commandment greater than these."

Mark 12:30-31

Love the Lord with ALL my heart, my mind, my soul, and my strength. I definitely was not doing that. Then He says, "Love your neighbor as yourself"... what does that even mean? I decided to do a deeper dive into this idea of love.

Many of us mistakenly believe that having an emotional attachment to others equates to love. Love is so much more than that. God created love to be an action.

When I didn't understand what love was, I deceived myself into thinking that going above and beyond—being a people pleaser—was what love looked like. Yes, I've read The Five Love Languages, and the way I show love is through acts of service, but there are limits to this thing.

I also believed that if I cared for people enough, they would reciprocate and treat me the way I treated them—or, as I now say, the way I deserved to be treated. Boy, was I mistaken—even when the evidence clearly said otherwise.

I can say now, I was disillusioned. And I was settling.

When we settle, we compromise our core values, beliefs, and how we desire to be treated and loved—all in favor of someone else's version of love or for their approval. Yeah, you might not think it's about approval, but deep down, it is… or acceptance. We let go of important aspects of our identity. We start sacrificing ourselves and neglecting our own needs, convincing ourselves that this is what love demands. Even when the relationship fails to foster personal growth or fulfill our hearts, we choose to settle for a definition of love that fails to satisfy our deepest desires or validate our inherent worth.

1 Corinthians 13:8 clearly and simply defines love.

Love is patient, love is kind.
It does not envy, it does not boast, it is not proud.
It does not dishonor others, it is not self-seeking,
It is not easily angered, it keeps no record of wrongs.
Love does not delight in evil but rejoices with the truth.
It always protects, always trusts, always hopes, always perseveres. Love never fails.

True joy can only arise from genuine love as defined by God. When we use God's definition of love as a measuring stick—monitoring and evaluating the relationships we choose to nurture—we find ourselves at peace with our choices and in greater harmony with our lives.

Life is meant to be enjoyed, and a life devoid of healthy, love-filled relationships cannot truly be joyful. Once we grasp and fully appreciate the essence of love—recognizing its value and impact on our lives and the lives of others—we will no longer settle for anything less than love in both giving and receiving. To compromise on this would undermine our "love" relationship with God, ourselves, and others.

Relationships—whether with self, romantic, family, friendships, or acquaintances—all require mutual regard to be sustainable and fulfilling. They cannot thrive if the regard is imbalanced, with one side investing more than the other. When the weight of regard becomes skewed, negative emotions and dissatisfying outcomes tend to burden the relationship.

In particular, women in lopsided romantic relationships often hold onto the belief that we can change our partners, prompting us to invest in mostly joyless and dissatisfying dynamics. We hope that our love will inspire the man to "level up," honor our efforts, and reciprocate our affection. After all, our situation is different from others: "He would never treat me the same way he treated…" These are the delusions we tell ourselves, as though we are uniquely special. I did, at least.

I was definitely one of those women who firmly believed in my own exceptionalism. I was convinced that my "specialness" could transform my "partner" (for want of a better word) from a toad into Prince Charming. However, it didn't take long—only six years—for me to learn the hard truth: I cannot change anyone. People must have an intrinsic desire to change themselves, driven by their own motivations. Change cannot be coerced or imposed externally; it must arise from within.

16

The same principle applies to all types of relationships. If family members, friends, or acquaintances are resistant to change and set in their ways, no external force or influence can alter them. As the renowned British/Irish playwright George Bernard Shaw famously stated, "Those who cannot change their minds cannot change anything." And let's not forget the most important relationship—the one with ourselves! If we are set in our ways, nobody can help us.

Did you know that *love* is mentioned in the Bible over 500 times? When God speaks to us about the fruit of the Spirit, the first one He mentions is *love*. Indeed, God's requirement for us is to love. This command encompasses love for Him, self-love, and love for others. It is both a divine mandate and a personal choice we make.

It is important to recognize that God's definition of love differs significantly from society's definition and the prevailing understanding of what love entails.

We will delve into an exploration and examination of some of God's characteristics of love, as outlined in 1 Corinthians Chapter 13. We will relate these qualities to our own lives, drawing from personal experiences and insights gained throughout my journey.

"Love is patient, love is kind. It does not envy, it does not boast, it is not proud. It does not dishonor others, it is not self-seeking, it is not easily angered, it keeps no record of wrongs. Love does not delight in evil but rejoices with the truth. It always protects, always trusts, always hopes, always perseveres. Love never fails."

1 Corinthians 13: 4-8

Love Is Patient.
Love Is Not Easily Angered

Whoah! That's a tall order!

Patience is a significant virtue that many of us fail to fully understand—or perhaps choose not to, especially when it comes to our relationships with those closest to us. I am particularly guilty of this, so I feel compelled to write about it.

One dictionary definition of the word "patient" is being able to accept or tolerate delays, problems, or suffering without becoming annoyed or anxious.

If you're anything like me, you may find yourself easily annoyed by even the slightest things, seemingly at the drop of a hat—especially with family and those closest to you. I don't know why, but it seems that I am often the least patient with the people who matter the most to me. Is it because I hold my family and loved ones to a higher standard, thinking they will love me regardless? Or is it because I tend to take them for granted, carelessly assuming they will tolerate whatever I throw their way? Food for thought—I don't have all the answers.

19

What I do know is that patience is a virtue I admire in others and desire to cultivate within myself. However, it can be incredibly challenging to practice and express. Impatience can be hurtful, not only to others but also to ourselves. It can undermine our values, principles, and even our faith.

Do the people who claim to love you truly demonstrate patience toward you? Or do they often resort to shouting or becoming upset, even over trivial matters? Do they dismiss you if you don't drop everything you are doing to accommodate them?

If they react strongly and lose their temper or are dismissive over small things, how do they handle more significant issues? Do they explode in fits of verbal and physical violence, resorting to hurtful and degrading words and actions? Are they displaying passive-aggressive behavior?

We use the phrase passive-aggressive often, but do we truly understand what it means? I think it's important to break it down.

Passive-aggressive behavior is a pattern of indirectly expressing negative feelings, often through inaction, moodiness, or lack of cooperation. Some signs of passive-aggressive behavior include:

Avoiding direct communication: A passive-aggressive person might avoid telling someone they're angry or hurt by giving them the cold shoulder, delaying a response, or pretending not to hear them.

Procrastinating: They might intentionally wait until the last minute to do something or make excuses instead of saying what's on their mind.

Being resentful: They might oppose others' demands or complain about feeling underappreciated.

Being sarcastic: They might respond to requests with sarcasm or subtle digs.

Denying their feelings: They might repeatedly claim that they are not mad or that they are fine, even when they are clearly not.

How should we respond to individuals, particularly those close to us, who consistently show impatience toward us, disregarding our feelings and expressing annoyance and irritation? Despite our efforts to respond with calmness, patience, and perseverance as God commands us, their lack of consideration can cause wounds.

Is it unreasonable for God to expect us to respond with love and patience toward those who are abusive to us and have wronged us?

It took me some time, but as my self-love grew, I came to realize a significant distinction between patience and tolerance. Initially, they may seem similar in nature, but upon closer examination, their differences become clear.

Patience involves the capacity to accept or endure adverse situations without becoming annoyed or anxious. It is the ability to remain calm and composed in challenging circumstances. Patience enables us to respond with kindness and forbearance, even when others act out of line or disrupt order. True patience entails enduring provocation and displeasure while responding with love.

On the other hand, tolerance has two meanings. One refers to the willingness or ability to accept the existence of opinions, attitudes, or behaviors that differ from our own. In my humble opinion, good tolerance, which is simply being respectful, is a virtue. I can be respectful of other people's opinions, even if they differ from mine.

Fun fact: I am mixed with almost every ethnicity one can think of. My family is a melting pot, which is why race was never a "thing" for me. I didn't see or really understand race until I moved to the U.S. for college. Anyway, I digress… My cultural influences, however, are Jamaican, Black, and Chinese.

When I think of attitudes and behaviors, I think of culturally different practices. For example, Asian people typically avoid direct eye contact and may gaze downward when talking because it can be seen as disrespectful to speak to someone while making eye contact. In Jamaican culture, I would hear, "Look at me when I'm talking to you!"

Asian cultures value collectivism, conformity, and social harmony. They encourage interpersonal relationships and interdependence. Western culture, on the other hand, encourages individualism and independence. Asians avoid shame, which is used as a mechanism to enforce social norms, societal expectations, and proper behavior.

I believe there are benefits to both, and for me, I have had the benefit of the balance of both. I have Indian friends who have had arranged marriages, and I have seen some work well and others end badly. It is not for us to judge other people's cultures. Some things may not work for us, but that doesn't mean we can't coexist in respect of each other's practices or beliefs, attitudes, and cultures.

Now, the other definition of tolerance involves enduring and accepting continued exposure to adversities inflicted by others, even when such exposure is harmful to our well-being. This is something I've lived through, and I have a passionate disposition against it. You are nobody's beating stick, and you are nobody's footstool! You are not here to tolerate people taking advantage of you, talking to you however they feel like, with no consequences. This applies to your personal and professional life!

This kind of tolerance can sometimes be motivated by fear, doubt, feelings of unworthiness, self-hate, pride, or other negative factors. However, it is rarely driven by love.

While patience and tolerance share some similarities, they offer distinct experiences. When we lack patience, we tend to respond unkindly. On the other hand, when we tolerate, our response may inadvertently perpetuate and enable unkindness to persist if left unchecked.

In our human nature, patience is a characteristic that many of us struggle with. Sometimes, we mistakenly believe that we are being patient when we stoically endure uncomfortable experiences. We may think that being patient means staying in relationships long after they no longer make sense. We may also make the misguided assumption that being patient requires us to tolerate things that we should have rejected from the beginning. However, when we view our responses through the lens of God's love, we come to realize that we were not actually being patient, but rather practicing tolerance at best. Hindsight is often clear, and we can now see the truth.

Looking back, I now recognize that I used to tolerate and even "forgive" an ex-boyfriend for the way he treated me. I would make excuses for his behavior, claiming that he didn't know any better due to his lack of prior experience with unconditional love. I would attribute his hurtful words or actions to stress or ignorance, convincing myself that he didn't truly mean them.

I would also become upset with my family and friends if they dared to discuss my relationship with him. I cut off communication with them regarding anything related to him. I believed it was none of their business to pass judgment on my choices and my way of being with "my man." I thought it best to keep them out of that part of my life, shutting out their perceived interference and choosing to deal with the situation on my own.

So, I continued to endure the abusive behavior, exercising all the "patience" in the world, while responding with "care and kindness." The more I sought to smooth over our differences (a.k.a. cater to his every desire), the more he continued to mistreat me. He unleashed his anger and bitterness upon me until I became toxic with despair. I isolated myself, grew scrawny, unhappy... Yet, I stayed with him.

At the time, I didn't realize that instead of being the patient and virtuous woman I believed myself to be, I was actually tolerating his behavior. I had a friend from Jamaica who was living in Florida at the time—he knew me before and during that relationship—and he said to me, "This is not the Catherine I know. The Catherine I know would never tolerate this situation." Who was I?

I don't know what happened. I guess all the insecurities I thought I had under control began manifesting in my poor choices. The truth is, I didn't love myself enough to demand love in return—neither from him nor from anyone else. I didn't believe I deserved to be treated any better. The patience I thought I was demonstrating was merely a disguise for the self-loathing I harbored within.

Fortunately, I have come a long way since then. I now understand and embrace the truth that the true source of love is God. Only through God's power can I truly love.

Thankfully, God provides us with guidance on how to love in 1 Corinthians Chapter 13. God's love empowers us to live a life of love—characterized by patience and kindness.

God's love within us enables us to embody a more excellent way of being. He requires us to be patient and respectful—but not tolerant of things that do not serve our growth or align with the purpose He created us for.

I believe in striving for excellence because that is what God calls me to do. For me, excellence means giving my best. When I love, I love wholeheartedly, with the utmost sincerity, holding nothing back. When I have expressed and given my best, it is enough, and I find contentment. However, there are times when, despite my best intentions, I may feel overwhelmed and frustrated, allowing negative thoughts to consume me.

We have the power to set the tone for how we are treated. We should not allow others to define our value, as their validation can also be revoked, leaving us with a sense of emptiness.

Now, how can you cultivate patience with others?

1. **Practice deep breathing:** When you feel yourself getting impatient, take a few deep breaths. Inhale slowly through your nose, hold for a few seconds, then exhale slowly through your mouth. This helps calm you down and regain a sense of control.

2. **Reframe your perspective:** Try to view the situation from a different angle. Ask yourself, "Will this matter in a week/month/year?" Putting things in a broader perspective can ease the urgency.

3. **Slow down your pace:** Many of us are in the habit of rushing through tasks. Consciously slow down your movements and speech. This can help you feel more present and less anxious.

4. **Practice mindfulness:** When your mind starts to wander or you feel impatient, gently bring your attention back to the present moment. Notice your surroundings, your breathing, or sensations in your body.

5. **Meditate regularly:** Meditation has been shown to increase patience and impulse control. Even just 5–10 minutes a day can make a difference. For me, I pray, listen to worship music, and reflect on God's Word.

6. **Manage your time wisely:** Poor time management can lead to impatience. Make a schedule, prioritize tasks, and build in buffer time between activities.

7. **Let go of perfectionism:** Striving for perfection can make us impatient. Focus on doing your best rather than aiming for flawlessness. I tell my students all the time: PROGRESS OVER PERFECTION!

8. **Be compassionate with yourself:** Everyone struggles with patience at times. When impatience arises, treat yourself with kindness and grace.

The key is to cultivate patience through consistent practice. With time and effort, you can become more patient in your daily life. What helps me is listening to worship music. Road rage was something I struggled with in Jamaica, so I developed the habit of listening to worship music while driving. It grounds me and reminds me who I serve. Exercise has also proven helpful—it's a great stress reliever and a healthy outlet.

As you contemplate the truth about what God requires of you in choosing love through patience, take the time to ask yourself these questions and answer them:

• In which areas do you need to be more patient with others?
• Who are the individuals you need to be more patient with?
• What changes do you need to make to exercise more patience with others?

Write down your responses; evaluate them, and be intentional about making the necessary changes. Remember, you are worth the effort.

Embrace the excellence that God intended for you. As you deepen your relationship with God, His love will compel everything you do, say, and desire. Enjoy your transformed life as you continue to love yourself more!

LOVE IS KIND.

"The world is full of nice people. If you can't find one, be one."

Nishan Panwar

Kindness is a critical attribute that reveals the force and nature of love. Living a life marked by kindness is one aspect of pleasing God.

The word kind is from the Greek chresteuomai, which means to act benevolently or treat someone as one's kin—one's own family.

Kindness is characterized by benevolence, tenderness, and a disposition that is considerate, helpful, humane, mild, and gentle.

While patience is a form of kindness, kindness primarily pertains to how we treat ourselves and others. It involves expressing love through goodness rather than bitterness, sharpness, or harshness.

Kindness is not solely about giving or receiving kind acts; it is about embodying a disposition of helping, enabling, and empowering others with positivity, care, and consideration.

In our communication with others, it is important to reflect on whether we are being harsh, critical, or judgmental—or if we are cultivating an environment of respect, love, and care.

God is love, and I am His creation. I am made in His image and likeness, which means I am love. I am created to give love and to live in love.

Love is kind. It's impossible to live in love and not show kindness. If you catch yourself being unkind, do a love check. If I'm aligned with God's spirit of love within me, kindness naturally flows. But if I'm not, I know I need to renew my spirit and realign with love.

Being kind entails treating ourselves with care, respect, and honor. It involves acknowledging our inherent value and recognizing the divine presence that resides within everyone. Through my relationship with God, I was able to clarify the true nature of love and how it should be expressed—within myself and toward others.

Under God's enlightenment, I honestly examined my role as a bearer of love, which inherently includes kindness. I evaluated whether I consistently demonstrated kindness. I also reflected on my response to those who do not show kindness—particularly those I love or who claim to love me—despite my kindness toward them.

As I examined my internal state of kindness under God's loving guidance, I realized that I fell significantly short. Let us not mistake kindness for generosity.

Kindness involves being generous without expecting anything in return, and acting out of compassion and genuine concern for others. Kind people are considerate, helpful, and mindful of other people's feelings. Kind people might:

- Give their time, money, and talent to support others
- Be patient and understanding (the one I struggle with)

- Show empathy toward others
- Use positive language and avoid hurtful comments (sometimes I don't realize I'm being harsh with my words and how I say things)
- Be non-judgmental and forgive mistakes

Generosity involves being willing to give help, money, or material things—especially more than would be expected. Generous people think about others and how they can improve their lives. However, generous people are not always kind. For example, a generous person may give a lot of money to support charities but be very ratchet in other aspects of life.

But His grace proved sufficient to restore His standard of love within me and give me the strength to navigate through any challenges I may face.

From this divinely enlightened standpoint, I became more capable of expressing love through kindness in areas I have struggled with—and continue to struggle with… but knowing is half the battle (IYKYK).

Now, what about those relationships in your life that you need to assess? Are the people you choose to allow into your life being kind to you? KIND — NOT GENEROUS.
Do they speak to you kindly? Treat you kindly? Do they give their time, money, or talent to support you? Are they patient and understanding of you? Do they show empathy when you need it? Do they use positive language and avoid hurtful comments?

Yes! We all mess up and can say hurtful things—but do they make a habit of it?

Are they non-judgmental and do they forgive your mistakes? Telling you the truth when you are messing up is them being kind. Beating it into you and reminding you of your stupidity is not them being kind—even if it comes from what they think is a place of love.

When you realize your stupidity, are they forgiving and non-judgmental? Do they continue to show care and concern for you?

You can nurture personal growth within yourself and foster positive, mutually enriching relationships with others.

Here are some ways to cultivate kindness with others:

1. **Practice active listening:** When someone is speaking to you, put down your phone, make eye contact, and focus on fully understanding what they are saying. This shows you value their perspective.

2. **Perform acts of kindness:** Look for small ways to brighten someone's day—like holding the door, giving a sincere compliment, or volunteering your time. Doing good for others can increase your own feelings of kindness.

3. **Develop empathy:** Try to imagine what it feels like to walk in someone else's shoes. Consider how they might be feeling and what they might be going through. This can foster compassion.

4. **Think about loving-kindness:** Visualize radiating kindness and compassion toward yourself, loved ones, strangers, and even difficult people.

5. **Surround yourself with kind people:** Spend time with friends and family members who model kindness. Their example can be inspiring.

6. **Be patient with others:** Recognize that everyone is on their own journey. Respond to frustrations with understanding rather than judgment.

7. **Cultivate gratitude:** Take time each day to reflect on things you are grateful for. Appreciating the kindness and goodness in your life can inspire you to pay it forward.

The more you practice kindness, the more natural and automatic it will become. Consistency is key when cultivating this important quality.

While contemplating what God expects of us when we choose to love through kindness, it is worthwhile to take a moment and ask ourselves these questions:

*   Am I kind to others?
*   Do I value kindness?
*   How can I be more kind?

Write down your responses. Evaluate them. Be intentional about making the change. You are worth the effort.

Live in the excellence that God intends for you to live. The more you grow in your relationship with God, the more His love compels everything you do, say, and desire. Enjoy your transformed life!

Love does not envy, it does not boast.

"Never underestimate the power of jealousy and the power of envy to destroy. Never underestimate that."

Oliver Stone

God has provided us with clear definitions of what love is—and what it is not. Two characteristics of what love is not are envy and boasting. Love does not envy, nor does it boast.

Envy can be defined as a feeling of discontent or resentful longing aroused by someone else's possessions, qualities, or luck (I prefer to say blessings). Through the Scriptures, God tells us that to envy is to be "conformed to the world." It means being solely focused on, and aspiring to, what the world—governed by mankind—has to offer. By conforming to the world, we limit ourselves and lose sight of the far greater blessings that God, from whom all blessings flow, provides.

In today's insta-world, envy is encouraged and promoted. We are constantly bombarded with images and stories of those who have more than us: greater accomplishments, more power, status, material possessions, beauty, better qualities and characteristics, reputation, or even perceived happiness. We are urged—and sometimes even compelled—to desire what they have at any cost.

It's considered acceptable, even admirable, to cultivate a competitive spirit and strive for a competitive edge over others. The principle of being satisfied with what we have is dismissed as outdated and irrelevant in today's culture. In America, we live on credit. We are taught to extend ourselves—go beyond our needs to our wants—not let anyone get the better of us, and always make ourselves look good. Generation after generation, the world's standards sow seeds of envy within us… Yah, I said it. You don't have to acknowledge it publicly, but we can't address something we aren't willing to admit.

To envy or be jealous is to express discontentment with who we are or what we have. Essentially, it's presumptuously telling God that He has shortchanged us. We declare that His providence is insufficient—that He is withholding blessings, and His distribution of them is unfair or unjust. We believe He could have done better for us. We feel like we've somehow been cheated because someone else is experiencing their season of breakthrough or abundance.

Envy can manifest in various ways—through anything we desire or perceive as lacking, which others possess or that we wish they didn't. This envy or "bad mind" (as we say in Jamaica) can even lead to harming the people we envy… and ultimately, it ends up hurting us.

In our pursuit to "keep up with the Joneses"—or in modern terms, "keeping up with the Kardashians"—we push ourselves to the limits of our physical, mental, and emotional endurance. We take on multiple jobs, academic programs, and social activities, all in an attempt to acquire more or outshine others.

"ENOUGH" isn't something we understand. And "staying in our lane?" Foreign concept. This desire to outdo others or even just measure up can lead to ego-driven tactics, underhanded practices, one-upmanship, and outright crimes that cause serious and far-reaching harm. We often "pretty up" envy with words like ambitious or driven, but what separates envy from ambition or drive is INTENT. What is fueling your ambition? Our motives matter.

Envy is destructive. It tears down instead of building up. It breeds bitterness, resentment, and discontent. It creates division, separation, and disunity. It's no wonder that one of the first characteristics listed of what love is not—is envy.

How can we identify envy in our lives?

- **Imitation:** They mimic your mannerisms—how you walk, talk, and dress. Some say "imitation is the greatest form of flattery"… but the difference is motive.

- **Comparison:** They frequently compare themselves to you.

- **Passive-aggressive behavior:** Subtle digs masked as politeness.

- **Backhanded compliments:** "Your flowers look lovely—even if they're not as colorful as mine."

- **Sabotage:** They try to undermine your success through rumors or quiet resistance.

- **Downplaying others' achievements:** They struggle to celebrate your wins.

- **Upset by compliments:** They become visibly uncomfortable when others are praised.

- **Fake compliments:** Their praise feels forced or disingenuous.

- **Rumor spreading:** They speak ill of others behind their backs.

I'm sure you can relate to many of these. Can you identify people in your life who exhibit these behaviors? They could be family members, co-workers, even people who call themselves your friends.

When we truly understand and embrace love, there is no room for envy or jealousy of others' blessings. When we genuinely love others, envy has no space to breathe.

Love rejoices with those who rejoice. It celebrates. It uplifts. It delights in the success of others.

"Narcissistic pleasure seekers routinely avoid developing the humility required to manufacture a life of full measure. Shallow persons such as me hide their insecurities behind a false persona of bravado, boasting of their inconsequential deeds, pyrrhic victories, and adamant refusals to tackle any task that they fear."

KILROY J. OLDSTER

Another characteristic that love is not is being boastful. Being boastful means showing excessive pride and self-satisfaction in one's achievements, possessions, or abilities. When we love as God requires us to love, we don't make idols of ourselves. Contrary to what the world advocates, we shouldn't elevate or promote ourselves above others.

This doesn't mean we shouldn't rejoice in our blessings. It's one thing to celebrate our gifts with others, but it's another to seek their praise and applause. In fact, it's healthy to affirm ourselves and think positively, but it becomes unloving and off-putting when we think so highly of ourselves that we become arrogant—viewing ourselves as superior to others or building ourselves up at their expense.

Being boastful can easily lead to arrogance. Arrogance can be rooted in narcissism or simply a lack of self-awareness. If you have someone in your life who you believe displays these tendencies—but you know their heart is good—consider sharing this insight with them. It might help them become more self-aware.

Some signs of an arrogant person include:

- **Overtalking:** Arrogant people tend to talk more than they listen and often assume others want their advice.

- **Centering attention:** They try to ensure conversations revolve around them and may feel agitated if they aren't the center of attention.

- **Taking credit:** They take credit for the work and achievements of others.

- **Difficulty accepting criticism:** They struggle to receive constructive feedback.

- **Lack of empathy:** They have trouble understanding or sharing the feelings of others.

- **Belief in their superiority:** They see themselves as better than others and may have an inflated sense of self-importance.

- **Disdain for other points of view:** They are often unwilling to consider perspectives other than their own—after all, they think they're always right!

- **Craving recognition:** They want to be acknowledged for their contributions but find it difficult to recognize or celebrate the efforts of others.

- **Winning at all costs:** Their desire to win isn't just about healthy competition—they want to win no matter the cost to others. (What do you value?)

God empowers us to love. And when we truly love, we reflect His nature and show the world who He is. So, when our attitudes and behaviors become prideful, self-absorbed, or ostentatious, we obstruct the beauty of God's love in us. Worse still, we can cause others to become less loving and less lovely.

As you reflect on what God truly requires of us when we choose to love and be loved, consider the people in your life who may struggle with envy, boastfulness, or arrogance.

1. Do you think others are envious of you? Who?
2. How can you encourage others to choose contentment?
3. Who in your life mistreats you because of their envy or arrogance?
4. Are they capable of change?
5. Are you willing to walk away from those relationships?
6. What steps do you need to take?

Write down your responses. Evaluate them. Be intentional about making the change. You are worth the effort.

Live in the excellence that God intended for you. The more you grow in your relationship with God, the more His love becomes the driving force behind everything you do, say, and desire. Enjoy your transformed life. Love yourself more!

Love Does Not Dishonor Others. It Is Not Self-Seeking. It Keeps No Record of Wrongs

Love is truly multi-faceted and multi-layered, as described in 1 Corinthians Chapter 13.

Love is the greatest gift God bestows upon us. In essence, it is the gift of Himself, as He is love. Each of us is created in God's image and likeness, and we possess His spirit of love within us.

Love is the pathway through which we enter a relationship with God. It is the road we must travel as we engage with others, and it is our choice to either express love or not.

The question before us is whether we will activate the pure love within us and allow it to govern our lives. To help us make this choice, let us examine some other aspects of what love is not.

Love Does Not Dishonor Others

Dishonor involves disrespect, tearing down or putting down others, and making them feel small or uncomfortable. It is a lack or loss of honor or reputation, causing shame, disgrace, acting unbecomingly, or being rude.

Dishonoring others is diminishing their worth and value. One can do this by calling people dishonorable names, gossiping about them, making unkind remarks, or holding a negative view of them. Dishonoring others is usually an attempt to elevate ourselves

In today's society, our language, behaviors, and attitudes have trended toward negativity. Everything is categorized as a challenge, frustration, or problem, and we are encouraged to be fiercely competitive. As a result, we often respond with righteous indignation to anything that threatens our survival or challenges our way of life. Society approves and justifies our defensive stance by claiming that we are merely protecting our space and being self-protective. These societal norms support the belief that we are justified in challenging individuals, groups, ideas, and situations that do not align with our viewpoints or positions. The highly valued "competitive spirit" pushes us to pit our intellect, capabilities, appearance, spiritual zeal, and other characteristics against one another in an effort to elevate ourselves and gain an advantage. However, these so-called societal norms are, in reality, promoting dishonor. Being negative, competitive, and dishonoring toward others under the guise of self-affirmation is not an expression of love.

One of my friends shared a story with me about her experience at the supermarket. She went to purchase a few items and joined the express checkout line. There was only one person ahead of her, but the transaction was taking an unusually long time. Impatient and irritated by the seemingly unhurried and inattentive behavior of both the cashier and the customer, my friend began to protest loudly and bitterly about the long wait.

Finally, it was her turn. As she approached the cashier, the previous customer—still packing her bags—turned to her and quietly said, "You could have been kinder, you know. Your outburst could have ruined someone's day."

My friend said she was stopped in the middle of a stinging retort by the truth in the young lady's words. That comment made her reflect on her behavior, which she realized had been unseemly, unloving, and dishonoring—to herself, to others, and to the God she professed to serve. She recognized the irony: she had gone to the supermarket on a mission of love, intending to gift a few items to someone, yet her impatience had betrayed that very love.

How can you tell if someone in your life is dishonoring you?

- Do they condemn you or others—putting them down, embarrassing them, or damaging their reputation?
- Do they act out of selfish ambition?
- Are they selective about who they treat with dignity and respect?
- Do they use personal attacks or dehumanizing language?
- Do they berate different perspectives?
- Do their words or actions bring people together or drive them apart?

I have come to know—and am absolutely sure—that living a life governed by love requires us to enter into and sustain a deeper relationship with God. The closer our relationship is with Him, the less likely we are to dishonor ourselves and others. To honor God and to love our neighbors as ourselves is to love ourselves more—by holding ourselves to a higher standard. Are we allowing others in our lives to dishonor us?

I was in an abusive relationship for years, repeatedly allowing not only that person to dishonor me, but also allowing others to witness me tolerate the dishonor—thus giving them permission to do the same. Through my actions, a standard of dishonor was established.

Love Is Not Self-Seeking

"Selfishness is not living as one wishes to live. It is asking others to live as one wishes to live."

Oscar Wilde

At face value, this quote helped me understand that love does not prioritize its own welfare or interests over those of others. Love does not pursue personal agendas or self-interests without regard for others' well-being. It is not self-serving, self-obsessed, or driven by selfish ambitions and desires. Instead, love serves others, bears their burdens, looks out for their interests, and seeks their welfare—even when personal sacrifice and self-denial are required.

The phrase *"love is not self-seeking"* reflects the idea that true love is not focused on personal benefit but on the needs and well-being of others.

In this context, *self-seeking* refers to being primarily motivated by personal gain, desires, or having one's own needs met. Love that is not self-seeking puts the other person first and is willing to make sacrifices for their sake.

Some habits we can cultivate to be less self-seeking include:

1. Putting the other person's needs and interests before your own, and being willing to make sacrifices or adjustments for their benefit.

2. Not expecting anything in return—loving without an agenda or strings attached.

3. Valuing the other person's well-being and happiness as much as (or more than) your own.

4. Being generous, kind, and helpful without concern for how it will benefit you.

5. Seeking to empower, support, and bring out the best in others, rather than simply satisfying your own desires.

In essence, *"love is not self-seeking"* describes a selfless, others-focused kind of love—one that prioritizes the good of the beloved, not just the gratification of the one loving. It puts the health of the relationship and the needs of the other person above self-interest.

*   **Others are valued more:** Love is not self-focused; it places greater value on others.
*   **Others are shown their value:** Love is expressed in ways that make others feel important and cherished.
*   **Others' needs are met:** Love is revealed in the consistent effort to meet others' needs and desires.
*   **Self-denial is practiced:** Love is demonstrated through laying aside preferences, comforts, or even one's life for the sake of others

It was incredibly difficult for me to imagine a world in which we all loved others before ourselves. Mind you, I agree that we are not showing love when we demand our way, trample on others' rights for the sake of upholding our own, or insist on having our due. I also agree that if we are not mindful, we can make idols of our interests and pursuits, compromising love. Moreover, I believe that an ego-driven, self-protective, self-seeking way of being will create barriers to fostering and maintaining positive, loving relationships with others.

It took me a while, but through the grace of God, I was able to recognize and appreciate the fact that love and self-seeking are polar opposites and cannot coexist. Equally, I was able to make the distinction between self-love, which dictates what pleases me, what I seek after, and what I want, and love that is rooted in humility and is always considerate of others. Love seeks not her own. Love is selfless.

In loving myself more, I do not deny others or place myself above them. Instead, I choose to be spirit-driven and embrace, express, and live out the love that God created me to do.

Love Keeps No Record of Wrongs

"Unforgiveness is like drinking poison yourself and waiting for the other person to die.." Marianne Williamson

If we claim to forgive but still keep a record of all the wrongs we have "forgiven," we need to question our intentions. Why do we hold onto that list of offenses? Is it to repeatedly torment ourselves or to potentially use it as ammunition against the person we claim to have forgiven?

Keeping a record of wrongs is like throwing out the garbage but storing it in a retrieval system for future use. What purpose does it serve? Over time, that stored garbage becomes toxic and detrimental to our well-being. Often, in an attempt to appear loving and forgiving, we tell our loved ones who have wronged us, "Let bygones be bygones!" However, as soon as another issue arises, we bring out the laundry list of past wrongs. Accusations fly, painful memories resurface, and the past is no longer left in the past.

I have personally experienced and understand how we can allow hurt to fester, creating a toxic and impenetrable barrier between ourselves and the person or people who have wronged us.

Have you allowed your record of wrongs—whether real or perceived—to fracture a relationship or hinder a sense of community? Do you constantly remind yourself that you are the victim?

Let's pause for a moment and acknowledge that concept—whether REAL or PERCEIVED. How many times have you been caught in a misunderstanding purely because of miscommunication, where you thought someone had wronged you? Let's remember that perception does not always equate to reality.

Not keeping a record of wrongs can feel unnatural. It's like having an uncomfortably itchy boil that we want to go away—yet we find satisfaction in scratching it. Whenever thoughts of the person or people involved arise, we remember the wrongs committed.

These wrongs may have caused personal, professional, or material harm— or perhaps they were simply an offense to our pride. Regardless of the grievance, we tend to store it, dwell on it, and sometimes even wait for revenge or some form of retribution, as if it were a register of unpaid debts.

We are human. We will make mistakes, jump to conclusions, and be "in our feelings." God isn't telling us not to feel; He is simply telling us that we can't live in those feelings.

We cannot truly love while harboring ill feelings against someone. We cannot love and hold their past wrongs against them as if it were a record of debts owed. According to God, this is not love. Love does not focus on the hurt, nor keep track of wrongs received—or, as Jamaicans say, "have it up in yuh craw (stomach)." Instead, it forgives.

Now, let me be VERY clear—this doesn't mean that those who have caused us harm should get a free pass or escape accountability for their actions. Nor does it mean we should tolerate or endure any and all forms of abuse under the pretext of love.

Loving someone does not negate the need for individuals to accept responsibility and face the consequences of their actions. In fact, we should encourage people to be accountable and support their spiritual renewal.

Love also doesn't subscribe to the notion of a "ride-or-die" relationship culture, which suggests that the abused person should endure the abuse in the hope that the abuser will eventually change. Love doesn't require us to be victims or enablers of soul-destroying relationships.

Sometimes, the most loving thing we can do is to love and forgive—but also release ourselves from the toxic aspects of the relationship without severing the bond of love with the person. In other words, it's a heart decision. We can love people from a distance. We wish them well. We do not carry grudges or hold onto resentment. Instead, we free our hearts from the burden of malice, let go of the past, reconcile our differences, and move forward with love.

We forgive the wrongs, release the pain, and embrace a future filled with a heart of love.

God's love requires us to develop and express a spirit of forgiveness, reconciliation, and restoration of wholesome relationships with each other, regardless of past wrongs. If the love is not reciprocated in action, we release them, pray for them, and be an example of what we expect.

With this understanding, it took some effort, but now I can honestly say that I can't think of anyone who has hurt me in the past whom I don't love today. I hold no grudges or malice. There is simply no space in my heart or mind for anything but love.

I may not forget a wrong, as there is a distinction between remembering and actively harboring or intentionally dredging up past wrongs to hold against someone. I do, however, know that I will not place myself in a situation to be repeatedly hurt, abused, or taken for granted.

Keeping a record of wrongs is disempowering. It robs me of joy, diminishes my capacity to love others, and prevents me from loving myself more.

Pray with me:

Father,

We thank You for Your grace and Your truth. We thank You for forgiving us for everything we have done that does not align with You and Your will.

We pray, Lord, that just as You have been gracious to us, You help us to extend that grace to anyone who has offended us or who will offend us. Give us a heart of love, a heart of forgiveness,

We release all offense to You; we pray for the wisdom to make the right choices in our relationships. Help us to release the things we need to release and the boldness to move forward aligned with Your will.

As Your word says, help us to be kind, tenderhearted, and forgiving to one another, as You forgave us, in Jesus name.

As you contemplate the truth about what God requires of you when you choose to love, it is worth taking the time to ask yourself these questions and answer them.

- Is there any way in which I bring dishonor to myself?
- Is there any way in which I dishonor others?
- Am I more focused on satisfying myself over others?
- Is loving myself more the same as being self-seeking?
- Do I keep a record of wrongs?
- Are there relationships I need to distance myself from?
- Are there reasons why anyone would create distance from me?
- Can I love and keep a relational distance at the same time?

Write down your responses. Evaluate them. Be intentional about making the change. You are worth the effort.

Live in the excellence that God intends for you. The more you grow in your relationship with God, the more His love compels everything you do, say, and desire. Enjoy your transformed life! Love yourself more!

"Love Always Trusts, Always Hopes, Always Perseveres. Love Never Fails."

Many of us define and interpret love in various ways, leading to different outcomes and impacts. However, as we now know (if we hadn't before), it is through God that the full nature and character of love are revealed. Without filtering love through God, it would be impossible to truly understand, appreciate, and fully express love.

According to the book *The Five Love Languages* by Gary Chapman, we all have different ways of giving and receiving love. Some of us may even have multiple love languages. Chapman explains that while the nature and character of love remain unchanged, we express and receive love in different ways. He identifies five love languages: words of affirmation, quality time, giving/receiving gifts, acts of service, and physical touch.

I agree with Chapman's perspective that love is a choice. We have the choice to love or not to love. When we choose to love, we align ourselves with God's way of love, which is constant and unconditional. Rejecting love means rejecting God's way and expressing ourselves in our own self-serving manner.

It's important to note that although we receive and express love in different ways, love should be present in all languages—how we speak to others, how we allocate our time, what we do with our gifts, talents, and treasure, how we serve, and how we physically express love through touch.

God's love inspires us to be inclusive and see no differences among people, except our common humanity. Love does not question who deserves to be loved; it is given freely and unconditionally. Love guides us to live in the Spirit, considering others and protecting their interests. It encourages us to overlook flaws, face challenges together, and enrich each other's lives.

God's way of love empowers us to give rather than receive, to trust, hope, persevere, and never fail to love.

Love Always Trusts

Trust is a critical element in every relationship—whether it's with family, friends, colleagues, or romantic partners. In fact, many consider trust to be the most important aspect of any relationship.

However, building trust can be challenging, and once it's broken, it can be difficult to regain. When trust is lost, it's only natural for people to be hesitant about opening up again. After all, no one wants to confide in someone only to have their secrets shared, nor do they want to trust someone's actions only to be disappointed.

I recall a time when I had a close friendship with someone I considered more than just a good friend—I considered her family. I later discovered that while I had been a loyal friend to her, she hadn't reciprocated that same level of friendship.

Some may call me naïve or foolish, but deep down, I knew there was an imbalance in our relationship. I chose to ignore it and brushed it off.

It's funny—when we are young, we don't think too much about friendship beyond having a good time and sharing life experiences. As I got older, I learned that friendship is a critical part of who we are.

My parents always used to say, "Show me your company and I will tell you who you are." I never fully understood or appreciated that until I got older.

Long before I came to that realization, this friend had consistently shown me, in various ways, that she didn't value our friendship as much as I did. One of her main character flaws was a lack of trustworthiness. Deep down, I knew this about her, but I didn't want to pass judgment.

Telling lies about insignificant things, choosing herself over our friendship—these are things I experienced on multiple occasions. Others who had also suffered betrayal by her shared their stories of hurt and pain with me. I would try to calm them by saying, "That's just who she is. You either love her or leave her." In hindsight, I can acknowledge how profound yet simplistic my thoughts were.

It absolutely was NOT okay for her to treat others with disregard, and it was NOT okay to tolerate it. BUT it was absolutely—and still is—our job to love her, even if from a distance.

Truth is, while I don't claim to be a saint myself, I strive to be a non-judgmental and forgiving person. I believe in accepting people for who they are and loving them unconditionally, regardless of their flaws or shortcomings. I have, however, grown to understand and appreciate boundaries.

I remember a time when my family was going through various challenges, and I visited one of my regular beauty salons. Someone there was able to tell me intimate details about my family's situation—details she had learned from that person.

What's more, this person proceeded to give commentary on my family's issues with such familiarity and confidence. She seemed to think she had the right because she'd been given preferred "second-row" seating to our problems.

Needless to say, I was mortified... and livid!

How could someone I trusted with my family be so callous and unmindful—to betray my family's confidence for the cheap thrill of gossip? I was beyond upset.

Now, I will tolerate almost any wrong done to me personally, but when it comes to my family—they are off-limits. To use a Jamaican phrase, "I will get brindle!"—meaning I will get "off the chain" angry and irrationally upset if you trouble my family. If you threaten or, worse yet, harm them in any way, shape, or form, the "glove" of love is off.

I felt a mix of negative emotions. I couldn't look past my hurt to fulfill the requirements of godly love. I knew I was at odds with my God, but I felt that person was undeserving of my love. The age-old adage, "Familiarity breeds contempt," seemed painfully true. The closer a relationship becomes, the higher the risk of disrespect.

My parents are warm and welcoming. Every house we've ever lived in has always been open to many. They're also very private—"old school," traditionalist types who value family and friendships. In fact, they rarely go anywhere or do anything unless it's with family or their few close friends.

Trust, loyalty, and confidentiality rank high on the totem pole of values for my parents. It was crucial to them to cultivate in us, as children, the importance of establishing meaningful relationships with people who share those same principles.

Here are the lessons I've learned from those trust violations:
- Not everyone places the same value on relationships as you do.
- Be mindful of who you let into your space.
- When someone shows you who they are, believe them.
- Forgive, but don't forget. Release it in your heart and move on.

I used to be the kind of person who trusted others until they gave me a reason not to. Now, I believe that developing close relationships requires getting to know a person's heart and intentions first. I'm hesitant to open up my trust indiscriminately. I believe it must be earned. To do otherwise would make me too vulnerable—I'm cautious about setting myself up for hurt.

Through God's grace, I've come to realize that regardless of people's intentions, every person is worthy of my love—even if I don't trust them.

Love is freely given, purely and simply. How it is received, and what others choose to do with it, should be of no concern to me. If they choose to take my love and trample on it, they'll answer to God. I'll take my lesson and love from a distance.

Trust comes from God. And at the end of the day, our trust is in Him. To love as God directs is to trust Him unconditionally—to trust that, regardless of the hurt or disappointments caused by others, He will always use it for our good. I've learned to ask myself, What lesson did I need to learn from this experience? How did God want to stretch me? I trust that God has a plan, and in time, I'll come to know what that is. I trust Him.

We have all had experiences of relying on, or placing our confidence and trust in, people who have repeatedly shown that they are not trustworthy or dependable. Yet, we keep expecting different results each time we entrust them with our confidence.

Discernment is important. We must strive to understand the hearts of the people in our lives. For instance, there is someone close to me who does not always set a guard upon her lips and seems incapable of doing so. She can be quite indiscriminate and indiscreet about what she shares with others.

Despite that, she is truly a lovely and loving person, and I don't believe she sets out to gossip with malicious intent. I think she genuinely enjoys sharing and believes she is being helpful—acting in your best interest—when she shares your stories with others, especially if it's happy news. She isn't trying to gossip or malign me.

She always expresses remorse and sincerely promises not to let it happen again. But honestly, I believe she can't help herself. Still, at the end of the day, she truly loves me and only wants what is best for me.

So, I chose to love her regardless—but I also decided not to share with her anything I am not ready for everyone to know. In doing so, I relieved her of the burden of deciding whether to share or not, along with the potential negative consequences. I enable her to remain faithful and true by not entrusting her with information I know she cannot keep to herself.

I decided to declutter our relational space, eliminating opportunities for betrayal, shame, blame, or distrust. I chose to honor her well-intentioned nature.

To honor others with our trust means projecting onto them positive qualities and values they may not currently possess but have the potential to develop, while using wisdom and discernment to know what they can be trusted with during that process of growth. As the German philosopher Goethe astutely stated, *"If we treat people as they ought to be, we help them become what they are capable of becoming."*

Love Always Trusts

Love always trusts means choosing to believe the best about someone and assuming their intentions are pure. It also means that love is not suspicious of the one it loves and is slow to believe damaging news. Love that always trusts is based on who God is, not on what others do. It is a willing sacrifice—there's no need to manipulate others to fulfill our needs.

When you choose to trust someone, you are being merciful and forgiving. People feel loved when they feel trusted and often rise to the occasion. Love that always trusts is not the same as being naive, undiscerning, credulous, or gullible. Nor does it mean lacking healthy skepticism. We are not to expect or demand that others must meet our needs or provide what we want before we offer our love.

Love Always Hopes

After a publisher read the first draft of this manuscript, she shared with me a story about her friend's response to the death of her child. Through the exploration and presentation of the meaning and application of "Love always hopes," her friend gained clarity about her own response to the tragic circumstances.

With the publisher's full approval, I can share the story as follows:

A young woman's seemingly healthy nine-year-old child suddenly fell ill and, within three days, was in critical condition in the hospital. By the third day, there was little hope for the child's survival.

Despite the pain she was undoubtedly experiencing, the Christian mother expressed a perspective that whether her child survived or passed away, it was all good because she trusted God's perfect will. She believed that with Him, *"All is well."*

One cannot help but be amazed by this woman's faith and trust in God, as well as her complete surrender to His will—even in the face of such immense pain. When asked how she could be so at peace and in harmony with God's will, the mother simply replied, "I have hope that if she dies, my daughter will be in a better place and that I will one day see her again."

While anyone who is a Christian accepts God's will and purpose and holds hope in redemption through Jesus Christ, the mother's response offers us a profound insight into the true meaning of hope and its connection to love.

Hope goes beyond mere wishes or desires; it encompasses full confidence and belief in a greater good. Hope is an expression of love because love always points toward a positive outcome in the future.

In the mother's case, her deep and unwavering love for God served as a lifeline that sustained her through grief. When her child eventually passed away the next day, her hope held her together. She did not fall apart in sorrow because her love for God—and her love for her daughter—assured her that all was well, and that death was not the final resting place.

As long as there is love, there will always be hope.

The impact of hope, which projects a positive attitude into the life of another person, is immeasurable. If you've ever had someone believe in you and share a hopeful outlook for your future, then you've experienced love that hopes. Part of showing love is hoping, and part of hoping is seeing the potential in others. When we love, we can always be hopeful and show confidence in others. Love roots for victory in others—for good to prevail.

The love that always hopes is focused on the bright side of life, desiring only the best for others. I thank God for the love that always hopes, as it brings out the best in me and empowers me to love myself and others more.

God wants us to have the same confident expectation for others that we have for Him.

* Expect the spiritual growth of others in Christ
* Treat people better than we may think they deserve
* Give people the benefit of the doubt
* Be hard to offend and easy to please

The Greek word for "hopeth" is elpidzo, which conveys an expectation of good things. It means looking forward to something with confidence and expecting it to come to pass. Rather than assuming failure or a bad outcome in someone's life, the agape love of God always expects the best in others. It not only expects it, but it is also filled with anticipation to see the manifestation of what is hoped for.

Love Always Perseveres, Love Never Fails

Endurance for the sake of endurance is not love. We are called to endure and persevere for what is right and to seek what is best for our loved ones and ourselves. We will delve deeper into this after exploring perseverance.

This entire passage is about a love that Jesus calls us to—a love that is often opposite of our feelings and natural tendencies. Paul also highlighted God's great attributes and what He empowers us to do. People gravitate toward those who encourage and move away from those who tear down and harm.

When we truly love as Jesus demonstrated and sacrificed for us to do, we reflect Him—we show Him to people who are hurting, damaged, and stuck in lives filled with worry.

We can bring healing and reconciliation, filling the emptiness of those whom others reject or refuse to see. The original call to the Corinthians was to show real love to a church that had forgotten how to love. We can follow that same call so that real love can be manifested in our lives, our homes, and our churches.

"Love always perseveres" means that love continues through both good times and bad. It doesn't give up or quit. The Bible uses the Greek word hupomenei, which means "remaining" or "enduring." Love endures life's challenges and remains steadfast. It respects others, even when we may be uncertain of their intentions.

Love roots for victory in others. Love wants good to win and truth to be revealed. Love perseveres through many trials—problems, misunderstandings, uncertainty, arguments, persecution, divorce, abandonment, lawsuits, being fired, and hurt. It's a decision of the heart. The Holy Spirit can sustain this love and help us grow in generosity and service to others.

When God tells us that love always perseveres, He means real love has staying power—it lasts. It doesn't fade or weaken. We can have confidence in God and faith in others, to hang in there and keep "going strong," especially in difficult times. Because God loves us so deeply, He stands with us—and even carries us through our struggles and disappointments.

Even when we feel we've hit rock bottom, when we are filled with despair, God is carrying us. My life is a living testament to this love.

Real love will never fade or become obsolete. It will remain standing when everything else falls apart. This love destroys rumors and gossip and helps us believe the best about each other—until proven otherwise by facts. It enables us to maintain relationships—with friends, family, co-workers, and our spouse—and not give up during times of intense stress and confusion.

Love carries us to the ultimate hope, pointing us to the cross and to eternity. This love reminds us that what we do and learn here on earth will echo into eternity.

This love is not based on selfish desires or mutual benefits. It aims to give rather than receive and must be expressed in thoughts, words, and actions. It is pure, true, and unbreakable. It endures to the end—and it forever loves.

I claim the truth of my being—that I am made in the image and likeness of God, who is love. By embracing this love, I love myself and others more, recognizing the oneness of our creation and the completeness of God's way of love.

Allowing love to persevere means not letting our circumstances harden us. Instead, we manage them through the grace of God and His love.

"Love endures all things" and "Love never fails" are both beautiful descriptions of God's definition of love—and both may feel difficult to live out. The Bible tells us love never fails. One translation says, "Love never ends." Love is a fundamental attribute of God, and because God is eternal, love is also eternal. Love will never fail.

Scripture reveals God's eternal love for us—a love that never fails, demonstrated through His suffering, death, and resurrection. Nothing can separate us from that eternal love. He reminds us in Romans 8:38–39 that neither death nor life, angels nor demons, the present nor the future, nor any powers, height nor depth, nor anything else in all creation can separate us from the love of God in Christ Jesus our Lord. In Jeremiah 31:3, God reassures us, saying, "I have loved you with an everlasting love." His love does not waver or falter.

As humans, our love is not perfect—but we strive for faithfulness and correction that comes from a place of love. I've been blessed with good people in my life who have shown me unconditional love in many different ways.

I know my family—despite our arguments—will always be there for me. I always have their best interests at heart, just as they have mine. I have friends who love me unconditionally yet hold me accountable, offering tough love when needed. That is a love that never fails.

I once believed I was in a romantic relationship built on love, but I later realized it was more of an obsession. Obsession is defined as "a persistent, disturbing preoccupation with an often-unreasonable idea or feeling."

I've had friendships where I invested time, effort, and resources that were never reciprocated. I discovered they were one-sided. These experiences taught me valuable lessons about the worth of my time and the nature of relationships.

It's interesting how we often see boundaries in a negative light, when in reality, God created them for our protection.

Let's go back to the beginning. Adam and Eve were placed in the garden and given freedom to eat from any tree—except one. Yet, we always seem to desire what we're told not to have. Is it because of FOMO (Fear of Missing Out)? As children, our parents warned us not to play with fire, but many of us still chose to learn the hard way.

Have you noticed that the things we "experiment" with are often done in secret? I used to hide and play with candles because I knew I'd face my parents' wrath if caught.

Returning to the beginning, Eve allowed Satan to tempt her into eating from the tree of the knowledge of good and evil. God had set a boundary—not as a restriction, but as protection.

Imagine a world without sickness, crime, or poverty. That's what could have been if obedience had prevailed.
Boundaries are essential. Choosing to be in relationships that reflect the principles of love as God intended is crucial. I've experienced many different kinds of failed relationships. I've mourned loss and endured the pain of rejection, feelings of lack, and unworthiness. Separation is painful—it was never part of God's original design for relationships.

Sometimes, the toxic fallout from these broken relationships makes it hard to embrace forgiveness—even in our spirit, let alone our actions. At times, rising to higher ground—cleansing and restoring our spirit—feels unattainable.

Sometimes, when the love we hoped for doesn't show up, we project calm, peace, and positive energy. We may appear strong and unbreakable—yet deep inside, we feel like we're falling apart.

I often asked myself: Did I fail to love? Or did love fail me?

Love fails to endure when my motivation is only about loving myself. Loving myself more means learning how to love others, how to show love, and how to receive love.

Take time to assess the people in your life who say they love you—and the people you say you love. Based on God's definition of love, can you still use that word?

As I reflect on "Love never fails" more deeply, I'm forced to ask: What motivates me? Am I always moved by love in my actions? From God's perspective, good actions without love as the motivation hold no value. It's not enough to simply do good and loving deeds. If they're not rooted in love, they're empty and meaningless. Even if they seem noble, they are worthless without love at the center.
Motivation, not just action, is at the heart of love.

In other words, when I'm motivated by love for others, I'll naturally express the characteristics of love—like forgiveness, patience, kindness—and avoid envy, boasting, pride, anger, or selfishness.

Love isn't just a checklist of qualities—it flows from a genuine shift in focus from ourselves to others.

Loving yourself more means understanding how you love others and how you want others to love you. It means knowing how you receive love and how you show it.

Love should not fluctuate. It should be steady and constant—a perpetual light in a dark world. Love is not based on whims, feelings, or fleeting emotions.

What changes do you need to make in the way you love others?

What changes do you need to make regarding the people who say they love you?

I've seen tremendous growth and blessings in my life—and in my family—by striving to consistently live out the characteristics of love.

STEP 2 - INTROSPECTION

I CAN DO ALL THINGS!

"Knowing yourself is the beginning of all wisdom."

-Aristotle

KNOWING WHO and WHOSE YOU ARE

The memo says, *"Love your neighbor as yourself."* It is a divine directive

Sadly, many of us did not grasp the "as yourself" part of the memo. Sometimes, we are our own worst enemy. Issues of insecurity, unworthiness, and self-disregard often hinder our ability to give and receive love. A lack of respect, regard, or belief in ourselves holds us back. Feelings of inferiority—as well as superiority—do not truly define us. We do not simply become who we think we are based on false self-perceptions.

The thoughts and inclinations of our hearts may shape our perceptions, attitudes, and actions, but they do not define who we truly are. The question each of us must ask ourselves is: who am I? As a critical follow-up, we must also ask: what do I choose to believe about myself in my heart? If the answer proves to be a conundrum, then perhaps you really do need to explore loving yourself more.

Sometimes, it's hard for us to see ourselves as God has created us: fearfully and wonderfully made! Each of us is unique and special—yet created in the image and likeness of God Himself!

God has placed in us the possibility to be, live, and express the greatness of who He is in us—and who we are essentially. Yet, sadly, we often shy away from claiming our birthright and affirming our greatness. Instead, we choose to dwell in the realm of limitations, where we diminish ourselves to fit into the narrow, soul-destroying parameters of "ordinariness," driven by fears, doubts, and an overwhelming sense of inadequacy.

Adverse circumstances such as abuse, discrimination, economic challenges, and more may have left us feeling as if we don't quite measure up to societal norms or meet others' expectations. Perhaps you frame your life and your world with a sense of lack, believing that you do not have or are not enough—not enough money, beauty, intelligence; not slim enough, shapely enough, sophisticated enough—or whatever other standards you or society deem as "enough." This is especially prevalent in the instant, comparison-driven world we live in, where comparison is at our fingertips.

For many of us, the spell of "not enough" seems to have been cast from various angles and sources at an early age, leaving us feeling powerless to break free. We were taught as children that our opinions didn't matter or that we weren't as pretty or as bright as other children due to constant comparisons.

Instead of trying to shake off the pressure of "not enough," many of us crumble under its weight and lose the will—or never realize—that we can rise from our limiting beliefs of "not-enough-ness" to claim and live out our greatness.

I grew up as a tomboy, loving the outdoors and spending time with boys, engaging in various outdoor activities like fishing and clay shooting with my grandpa. Playing "Dolly House" or embracing girly fashion was never my thing.

As I got older and my girlfriends became more "girly" in their style choices, I distanced myself from it all. Looking back, I realize it was because of my insecurity and uncertainty about myself—feeling that I didn't quite measure up.

So, what made me so insecure? As an adult, after much therapy, I can now acknowledge that it had something to do with my relationship with my father. I love my father. Subconsciously, I sought approval from him.

Although my parents were together, my father—being a pilot—traveled frequently for work. He was physically present, but there was an emotional distance between us. He played the role of the disciplinarian rather than the nurturing "Daddy" figure I unknowingly yearned for. I always felt like I fell short in some way and that nothing I did was good enough or measured up to his expectations.

I developed a belief that my father wanted me to be "more," but I couldn't quite define what that meant. Consequently, I settled into the feeling that something was lacking within me, and I perceived myself as less than others. In the gap between my interpretation of who he was and what I wanted him to be, I formed a false sense of not being "good enough."

My father was oblivious to my emotional struggles and the role his interactions with me as a child played in fostering my self-doubt and low self-esteem. I was trapped in my internal prison, suffering silently. No one knew of my desperate need for love and acceptance—and even if they did, neither they nor I would have known how to fulfill it.

This purgatory-like state of feeling unlovely and unlovable, coupled with the profound discomfort it brought, stayed with me throughout my journey from childhood into adulthood.

It didn't help, too, that physically, I didn't have a good impression of how I looked. My hair was too short. I was super skinny (so much so that one uncle called me "wingey," and the other called me "mawga"—two Jamaican words suggesting that there wasn't "enough meat on the bones").

I just generally felt aesthetically unpleasing in my physical appearance— quite like the "ugly duckling"—and considered myself a social misfit. Some people even mistook me for a boy. In my all-girls Catholic high school, I played the role of the "husband" in a mock wedding, which further affirmed my belief that I wasn't "good enough" to be considered for the role of the "beautiful" bride or even a bridesmaid.

Throughout my elementary/prep school, high school, and college years, I hung out with all the "hot girls"—the beautiful and popular ones—yet, I never considered myself one of them. They tried to change that. They dressed me up whenever they had the chance. They tried to make me "beautiful." However, I knew deep down that their efforts were in vain. No matter what they did, I didn't feel beautiful.

Now I understand the truth: no matter how much we dress up on the outside, if we feel ugly and unlovely on the inside, it's all a façade, and the true value of those efforts is lost.

We often say that beauty is an inside job. Well, I believe "hotness" is an inside job too!

During my adult years as a working woman, there was a period when I occasionally wore dresses to work. Whenever I did, it would create a stir in the office because people weren't accustomed to seeing me in a dress. Naturally, the more I wore them, the less of an impact it had—until it became more of an expectation.

I once shared with a girlfriend that I sometimes wished I were one of those women who dressed up every day and confidently strutted their stuff, exuding self-assurance and panache. I admire women who present themselves well. They radiate confidence, self-assurance, and a sense of belonging. Their presence commands attention. They seem to be in control of their lives and affairs, with a regal certainty, knowing they truly rule their world.

Confidence is indeed an inside job—but my inner self lacked it. My girlfriend asked me, "Why not? Why can't you dress up like those women you admire? Why do you dim your shine?" I responded to her, saying, "I can't be bothered; it takes too much effort."

The truth is, as I explained to my friend, I didn't actually want the attention. Drawing that kind of attention to myself made me feel exposed and vulnerable. I feared it would subject me to unwanted scrutiny and possible criticism from others, which would only heighten my anxiety about my perceived failures and inadequacies. It would further solidify an already deeply rooted negative perception of my self-esteem.

My girlfriend—who is now also my business partner—turned to me and said, "Seriously? Does that sound like someone who lives in excellence?" OUCH! Funny how God places people in your life to keep you honest and to speak truth to you.

I remember doing a photoshoot for my friend. He was a photographer, and his sister was a makeup artist. They were creating a portfolio for her work. I agreed because the pictures were for them—it was to showcase their work. It wasn't about me.

I remember getting the pictures and sending them to the person I was seeing at the time. He commented that my sister looked beautiful. I smiled and said, "That's me." He immediately responded that I had on too much makeup and he didn't like it. LOL.

Many years later, those same pictures were shown to a gentleman who became interested in courting me. The short version of the story? We ended up encountering each other at my neighbor's house one evening and decided to go out for a meal. I was dressed in sweatpants or jeans and a T-shirt, as per usual—quite disheveled. After all, I'm a girl of comfort.

While eating, he pulled out his phone, showed me the pictures, and remarked that he had received those photos of me... and I didn't quite look the same. LOL.

This time, with a heart that had learned to love myself more, I was able to laugh. It was undoubtedly a laughable moment. His ungracious and uncharitable comment didn't offend or wound me in the least. I found it more amusing than anything else.

Empowered and emboldened by the spirit of loving myself more, I responded to him, saying, "Well, honey, this is who I am! If the girl in the picture is who you want and are looking for, then you're wasting your time with me!"

I will never be the girl who wears makeup every day. Not just because I don't know how to apply it (trust me, I've even taken classes), but because I couldn't endure it all the time!
Mind you, now I do make an effort to get dressed—even if I still prefer wearing jeans. I do care about the impression I make on others with my "style" choices, purely because I know that I am a representation of God. And He is a God of excellence. So, no matter how simple, I make an effort.

What matters most to me is living the truth that knowing who I am—and whose I am—should be reflected in everything I do, say, and embody.

I am the child of the King!

I am fearfully and wonderfully made.

I am created in His image and likeness.

I am made perfect the way I am . . . special and unique.

I am created with the greatness of God within me.

"We are what we believe we are."

C.S. Lewis

I remember one day walking into my girlfriend's birthday dinner, and without realizing it, my head was down. A powerful woman, who is like a mother to me, exclaimed, "No! No! No! You walk right back outside and re-enter with your head held high and your posture in good order! Don't you ever walk into a room with your head down."

From that moment onward, I committed to owning and exuding the confidence that comes only from claiming the God-given greatness within me.

Now, when I walk into a room, I walk tall. As a child of the King, I am assured of my value, worth, and impact.

I am a child of the King—greater than the trees and the stars... I have a right to be here!

What steps did I take to change my mindset about who I am?

1. I GOT TO KNOW MYSELF!

I know who I really am, and more importantly, I know who my God—my Creator—says I am and who He says I was created to be.

I implore you to get to know yourself! Invest time in exploring and discovering who you are—what you believe, value, and enjoy. What drives you? What are you passionate about? What matters to you? What are your likes and dislikes?

It's impossible to love yourself if you don't even know who you are. When you truly get to know yourself, you will be able to accept, love, and honor yourself.

2. I IMMERSED MYSELF IN DEEP AND THOROUGH SELF-EXAMINATION

I explored every aspect of my being: my strengths, weaknesses, vulnerabilities, sensitivities, values, and my vision for life. I delved into everything! No area was left unexplored.

It has been an exciting, albeit occasionally uncomfortable, journey of self-discovery. With my newfound self-awareness, no one can define me except me. I know myself! It has taken me years to write this book, and I still frequently engage in this exercise as I navigate different seasons and stages of life.

3. I AFFIRM MYSELF

I know who God says I am, and I know who I am.

I'm aware of my strengths, gifts, potential, and excellence. Each day, I make a conscious choice to nurture my greatness with a growth mindset and to embrace the positivity that comes with it. I acknowledge that I am a work in progress and am intentional about growing every day.

4. I READ A LOT

I have developed a deep love for learning—through books, podcasts, TED Talks, and more. I especially devote myself to studying the Bible and related inspirational literature, seeking to deepen my understanding of life as our Creator designed it.

In addition, I enjoy personal development books. There's so much to learn from others! While I may not excel in every area, I can certainly learn from those who do.

I love books that bring about breakthroughs—not just insights or minor improvements, but powerful, lasting results that unfold and expand over time.

It's through intentional development and reflection that I've been able to recognize, claim, and unleash my greatness—and help others do the same.

5. I EMPOWER OTHERS

I strive to help others recognize and release the greatness within them— the greatness they were created to walk in. I aim to empower them to love themselves more.

In the process of helping and empowering others, I experience growth and fulfillment. I learn to appreciate and love myself more. This reciprocal flow of love is a testament to the power of God's love.

6. I VALUE AND HONOR THOSE WHO LOVE AND SUPPORT ME

I've made a conscious effort to appreciate and cherish those who genuinely love me—instead of taking them for granted or treating them carelessly.

I stopped prioritizing people who didn't deserve my time and attention over those who truly cared for me.

I now embrace and stay close to those who love me unconditionally, through both the highs and the lows. These are the people who have always been honest with me and gave me tough love when I needed it.

7. I LIVE IN PERSONAL INTEGRITY

With personal integrity, I live a more meaningful and authentic life. Personal integrity means being honest with yourself, acknowledging your limitations, and following through on your word—no matter what. It is one of the most important, yet often overlooked, forms of integrity.

It empowers me to achieve my goals and live my best life. And remember— your best life can only be defined by you. What does that look like for you?

8. I LIVE A LIFE OF MEANING AND PURPOSE

I create new possibilities and take steps to make them happen. I believe I'm capable of achieving whatever I put my mind to.

I am empowered to choose an extraordinary life—one of harmony and well-being—led with confidence, creativity, and care for myself and others.

In relationships, leadership, and every other aspect of life, I strive to see meaning and purpose manifest—not only in my life but in the lives of others.

9. I LIVE IN GREATNESS

I live in freedom, at peace with who I am, and I embrace the power to be effective in the areas that matter most to me: the quality of my relationships, my purpose, my personal productivity, and my well-being.

I live with confidence, enjoying and celebrating life while making a positive impact on others.

10. I LOVE MYSELF MORE

When I love myself more, I remove from my life anything that isn't healthy for my well-being—whether it's people, jobs, beliefs, or habits. I let go of anything that makes me feel small, inadequate, or "not enough" and doesn't add value, edify, or enhance my life and purpose.

Loving myself more enriches me with self-confidence, self-worth, and positivity. It means seeing myself as whole, complete, and deserving of nothing less than the best life has to offer. Many of us find it easier to love others than to love ourselves. Sometimes we're critical, harsh, and even abusive toward ourselves—fostering toxic habits, unhealthy relationships, and distorted perspectives about life.

But it's time to rise from every unworthy place and embrace our full stature as children of God—loving, respecting, and honoring ourselves accordingly. Loving oneself isn't about being self-absorbed or narcissistic. It's about valuing yourself as God's creation and recognizing the beauty and greatness of His image and likeness within us.

In all areas of my life, I will not dishonor myself. I will honor and affirm the greatness and excellence within me—coming purely from God, the I AM. This is a daily effort. It doesn't come naturally to me, but it gets easier each day to celebrate my wins and embrace who I am—and who I am becoming.

I am a motivational teacher, thanks largely to Mrs. Cortia Bingham McKenzie—an inspiring and truly great woman who saw my potential and was unrelenting in her mission to help me realize it. She encouraged me past my fears, opened my mind and voice, and filled my heart with the courage to share my gift of public speaking with diverse audiences.

What Mrs. McKenzie did for me, she has done for many others. She continues to inspire thousands of women and young girls, empowering them to express themselves boldly and confidently as effective public speakers.

I am a connector with an extensive network and an uncanny ability to connect people, brands, and businesses.

I am a leadership and growth speaker, trainer, and coach. I invest a great deal of time and money into developing and honing my training, coaching, and facilitation skills.

I am certified by the internationally renowned John C. Maxwell. His passion for leadership and growth, fueled by his love for God, mirrors my own. His focus on helping others, particularly youth, serves as a perfect blueprint for me.

I am a mentor to many, enabling them to recognize, claim, and live their greatness through self-exploration, goal setting, guidance, motivation, emotional support, and role modeling. I am blessed to be a blessing to others.

I am a woman who loves myself enough to choose to live a balanced life. Balance doesn't mean having it all together but rather maintaining an inner sense of peace and calm regardless of life's challenges.

Despite being busy, I prioritize making time for God, myself, and activities that bring me joy, satisfaction, pleasure, fulfillment, and rejuvenation.

I have chosen to exercise the power to create harmony between my responsibilities and myself. I recognize that there is a time and place for everything, and certain seasons may require more time and effort in specific areas of my life.

I am confident in receiving, giving, and sharing love and affection with others. I have found the love of my life, and I can proudly claim and express it without fear or insecurity.

I am confident in the mutual love we share. I know that our beautiful togetherness would not have been possible if I hadn't learned to love myself.

You see, I had become afraid of letting anyone get too close and exposing my vulnerability. I didn't want to be a victim of someone else's power, control, and presumptions of dominance. I didn't want to be hurt again.

My relationship with God enabled me to break through my fears and self-defeating thoughts, attitudes, and behaviors, leading me to love myself more.

From the vantage point of loving myself more, I have been empowered to open up fully and embrace my husband for all that he is.

I thank God for blessing me with a godly, good man.

I am blessed, knowing and living my true identity as a child of the King.

With this awakening to my identity, I receive and embrace my birthright gift to love myself fully.

I treat myself as someone I deeply and completely love in my thoughts, actions, words, choices, and relationships with others.

In loving myself, I focus on all that I am!

I express the greatness and love of God in me.

I am created to shine, to be a light in the world.

I am created to live with purpose and fulfill the purpose that God has created me for.

I live in love! I love myself more!

Consider these questions:

- Are you harboring limiting thoughts that get in the way of loving yourself and living a transformed life?

- What are some of the limiting thoughts you need to change?
- As Romans 12:2 says in part, "Be transformed by the renewing of your mind. Then you will be able to test and approve what God's will is—his good, pleasing and perfect will."
- Indeed, it is in the renewal of the mind that transformation takes place through God's good grace.
- Who are you? What are the things you know to be true about yourself?

"Do not be yoked together with unbelievers.
For what do righteousness and wickedness have in common?
Or what fellowship can light have with darkness?"
—2 Corinthians 6:14

What does it mean to be unequally yoked?

The term "unequally yoked" originates from ancient biblical times when two oxen were joined together with a yoke—a wooden beam placed around their necks, allowing them to be teamed up to work in unison.

An unequally yoked team consisted of one stronger ox and one weaker, or one taller and one shorter. The weaker or shorter ox would walk more slowly than its stronger, taller counterpart, causing the load to veer in circles. When oxen are unequally yoked, they cannot complete the task set before them effectively.

This same principle applies when we team up or pair ourselves with people who, for various reasons, cannot create the balance necessary for fruitful and fulfilling relationships.

Many associate the term "unequally yoked" with romantic relationships, particularly marriage. However, it's time we broaden our perspective and realize this principle applies to every kind of relationship in our lives—family, friends, colleagues—everyone!

While we are all called to love, serve, and live in right relationship with one another, we are also advised in 2 Corinthians 6:14-15 not to be unequally yoked. Though the Apostle Paul speaks to a deeper spiritual reality—warning God's people against yoking with those who serve other gods—the principle is also applicable in other aspects of life.

Let's consider our relationships. Imagine one part of the yoke around your neck and the other on someone else's shoulders. If you're the lead ox, you should determine the bearing, pace, and path. Through your yoke, the other person in the relationship should feel your direction and follow accordingly. The roles may be reversed at times, but the principle remains: both must be pulling in the same direction for the partnership to work.

Are the people in your life bearing their share of the weight, journeying with you in love and nurturing? Or are they constantly taking, draining, and burdening you? Does their yoke bind you together as a team—or pull you apart?

There was a young lady I once considered family. I regarded her as a "big sister" and loved her dearly. When I had to travel out of the country for a while, I entrusted her with my car and cell phone. That's how much I trusted her. To my dismay, upon my return, I discovered that this "dear sister/friend"—in whom I had placed so much trust—had used my phone to message Mark, telling him all kinds of negative and personal things about me. I was deeply hurt by this betrayal. Still, I chose to forgive, forget, and move on.

Years later, this same "sister/friend" began dating one of my ex-boyfriends shortly after we had separated. What hurt the most was that, during and after the relationship, I had confided in her about our struggles and sought her advice. Imagine my shock upon finding out she was dating him. She had been listening to my heartaches, giving me counsel, and then practically moved into his house after the breakup—under the guise of "looking out for me." That felt like the ultimate betrayal.

When I confronted her, she replied curtly, "There is nothing to talk about!" That told me all I needed to know—just in case I'd missed it before.

There was no more denying the truth: I had placed far more value on our relationship than she had. I was laboring under the illusion of a deep friendship, while she had never even taken a step toward true friendship. That realization hurt to my core, but, as always, I forgave and moved on.

Some people thought, and some still believe, that our relationship ended because she got involved with my ex. But the truth is, it had already been broken—imbalanced, awkward, and impossible to sustain. I had claimed her as a friend, even elevating her to "sister" status, but she had only gone along for the ride. We were unequally yoked.

I still love her family and remain in touch with them, but I am completely detached from her. It's not that I don't love her—I do—but I love myself more, enough to let her go. I thought I was a great friend to her, but she never truly reciprocated. We were unequally yoked for the journey of friendship.

Even now, years later, I sometimes reach for the phone to call her—usually on her birthday. Then I catch myself and put the phone down, remembering that my friendship held no real value for her. But I matter to me, and now I make choices that reflect self-love.

Betrayal is something we all face at some point. Naturally loving and trusting people are especially vulnerable. It's as if we attract hurt and deception like a magnet.

I once had a coworker who served as the general and human resource manager at an organization I worked for. I had known her before I joined the company, and I was excited to work with her. Her boss constantly sang her praises, and I looked forward to being part of her team.

We worked well together—or so I thought. I would bring up issues and suggest improvements, which we'd discuss and agree on. I believed we were a great team.

One day, I told her I planned to speak with the managing director about a proposal to increase compensation for the distribution team. She said she had raised the issue many times to no avail, but encouraged me to go ahead and try.

To my utter astonishment, when the managing director called her into the meeting, she said she didn't think the proposal was a good idea and that it wasn't necessary. I couldn't believe my ears. This was the same woman who had supported and encouraged me just days before!

Thankfully, the managing director approved the proposal and the changes were implemented. But that moment marked the beginning of the end of what I thought had been a trusting, mutually respectful relationship.

I could go on with more stories of false "friendships." The truth is, I've always left myself wide open—vulnerable to repeated betrayal from people I believed I shared a close bond with.

But here's what's also true: I neither have the capacity nor the desire to stay angry with anyone. I forgive easily, forget even more easily, and move on readily.

Now, by God's grace and through His Word, I filter my relationships and the roles I play in them. His guidance helps me attract and nurture relationships that are positive, balanced, and mutually enriching.

Had I understood the principle of not being unequally yoked earlier, I would have saved myself much grief. I would have enjoyed greater joy and peace from relationships grounded in mutual love, values, and regard.

From all these experiences, I've learned:
- Loving yourself more means being intentional about who you allow into your life and recognizing when it's time to create distance.
- While we should love and care for everyone, we must be cautious about empowering people who can greatly influence the direction of our lives.

- Surround yourself with people who share your values and contribute to your life as much as you contribute to theirs. Remember, iron sharpens iron.
- Pay attention to character. When people show you who they are— believe them!

Ultimately, God is the leader of my life. It is through His direction that I find my bearing, pace, and path. By following His yoke, I work effectively as part of His team—and all things come together for my good.

Please take time to reflect on this important principle: Do not be unequally yoked.

As you reflect, think about each relationship in your life and consider these questions:
- Is your relationship—personal, professional, or otherwise—equally yoked?
- Is one person constantly taking while the other keeps giving?
- Do you share similar beliefs and values?
- Are you both moving in the same direction?
- Are you both motivated and driven by similar goals?
- Do you encourage and support each other to grow and improve?
- Do you both exhibit qualities worthy of mutual respect and admiration?
- Is your relationship more of a hindrance than a help—spiritually and emotionally?
- Does it fill you with joy and peace, or leave you feeling stressed and broken?

Remember, Jesus says, "My yoke is easy and My burden is light." We can always look to the Father, through Christ, to guide us toward equally yoked relationships—and give us the strength to walk away from those that are not.

Love yourself enough to be free from the burden of unequally yoked relationships.
Seek, nurture, and maintain only those that are balanced and life-giving. You deserve to move forward in harmony with God's promise of abundance.

Claim the promise!

INTENTION

The Two Words at the Heart of the Gospel
It marks God's relentless, merciful interventions in human history
It teaches us that God does not wait for us to bring ourselves to him
But that he acts first.

—Casey Lute

The word "but" is such an important conjunction—especially in the context of who God is.

But God works in our present age, just as He has in all the past and present ages, and He will continue to work in the ages to come.

But God works for me, just as He will work for you. But God works for my good and comes through for me—every time!

But God is sovereign and can work all things together for good.

But God can turn ashes into beauty.

So many times, I found myself mired in circumstances where I had no hope, no power to rescue myself, no ability to even try on my own. But God...

At one time, I bought a brand-new Toyota Corolla—my first car purchase. I had it for about a year and a half before I gave it to my brother because his car was falling apart. He had a 1992 Acura (as I recall), a motor vehicle with duct tape on the side mirrors and a towel in the car, ready for use in case it rained—because the roof leaked.

I bought myself another car—a brand-new Nissan Murano. My parents then took the Toyota Corolla, which was barely two years old, from my brother and traded it in for a new Honda Accord.

I was so upset! How could my parents do that? As Jamaicans would say, I "carried belly" over that car—which means I was well and truly angry. To think my parents took my car and traded it in without even a conversation. Let's be real—I went with them to choose the Honda—but I hadn't yet processed that they were trading in a car that I had "gifted" to my brother.

Years later, I found myself on my face, bawling my eyes out on my bathroom floor. It was in that moment that all the things I already knew came flooding in. I realized that my ex-boyfriend had become my god. My life revolved around him, his family, and his business.

Quite frankly, I gave my ex more time and effort than I gave to God, myself, my family, or my friends. It was as if he was a fog machine—clouding my internal view of balance and reality—leaving just a small portal through which I could only see him and give him my full attention. But God sees through our foolish ways, reaches us through our stubbornness, and guides us to His will. God cleared my fog, and I snapped into reality!

There I was, claiming I lived to love and serve my God, but I was not living like His child. I certainly wasn't living like a citizen of His kingdom. If I were, I would have been obedient.

I knew that living in obedience to God in all things demonstrates love and respect for Him. I knew that obedience is a key part of a Christian's relationship with Christ—yet my actions, whether intentional or not, revealed my disobedience.

I was always going to church, praying, and reading His Word. But I wasn't drawing near to Him or growing in my relationship with Him, because I was not acting in obedience to His will or directions.

As a Christian, I knew I had no choice but to "shape up and ship right" in my walk with God—and that meant obedience.

God blessed me immensely once I resolved in both heart and mind to renew a right spirit within me and be obedient to Him in thought, word, and—most importantly at the time—deed.

Shortly after proclaiming my resolve to be obedient and live in God's will and purpose, I received a phone call from Jamaica with a job offer from a major multinational company. I hadn't lived in Jamaica for over twelve years. I hadn't even applied for a job there! Why would I be shortlisted for such a role? On top of that, the job was in marketing—and I had no formal education in that field. I had never worked for a big corporation— let alone a multinational! So how was this all possible? All I can say is—but God. But God knows you. But God knows your heart. But God knows your needs and desires.

I serve an awesome God! I live in the power of the "BUTS" God has placed in my life and circumstances. But God.

Do you remember that same car I told you about earlier? The one I was so upset about and "carrying belly" over? My brother drove from Colorado to Florida in that same car to give it back to me—after my own car was repossessed. But God.

And that house I had that was up for foreclosure? My best friend's sister bought it! I didn't end up with a foreclosure on my credit. But God.

When God shows up, He shows out! Nothing and no one can deny that it was all God. The Bible tells us that if we are His, we are already overcomers. When we are His, we triumph over the worst that can be thrown at us. When we are His, we can live free and clear of worry, knowing that we can cast all our cares upon Him. When we are His, we can love ourselves more—knowing that He loves us and will guide our path toward the greater good.

God has a perfect plan for each of our lives. We just have to be willing to claim and fulfill that plan through a relationship with Him and obedience to His will. I know I could never have recognized or claimed the "but God" moments in my life had I not chosen to live in obedience to Him.

As I had to ask myself, I urge you to ask yourself these questions:

- Are you obedient to God? If not, are you ready to be obedient?
- What areas of your life do you need to submit to God and be obedient in?
- What are the chains or bondages in your life that need to be broken?
- What are the situations from which you need to break free?
- What are the limiting choices that you need to put a stop to?
- Are you ready and willing for God to do a new thing?

Think of the times your faith was tested by circumstances that knocked you off your feet—but God showed up, and you realized He was all you needed to keep going through your darkest hours. It's in those moments that "but God" means everything.

I celebrate my "but God" moments and pray that you, too, will find much to rejoice in when you reflect on yours.

I rejoice in all the but God moments I've experienced in my life, and I am humbled and thankful that He rescues me—even when I'm in the deepest pits of despair, fear, and confusion. He always comes through for me—mightily!

But God is sovereign and can work all things together for good.
I had no hope on my own, no power to rescue myself, no ability to even try. But God.

It's important to remember that I had to be open, willing, and obedient in order for God to move in my life. But God. Just trust and obey.

Love yourself enough to be obedient. Live life confidently and triumphantly, knowing that He is... but God!

STEP 3 - MINDSET

I CAN DO ALL THINGS!

"I can do all things through Christ which strengthen me."
—Philippians 4:13 (KJV)

rowing up, the Bible didn't appeal to me. Reading it was a tedious and laborious process. I couldn't get through the "thous" and "shalls," and I didn't even attempt to understand anything. If reading was enjoyable (which it is now), the Bible was the opposite for me. It just didn't have the appeal to make me want to read it.

If only I had known and understood then what I know now—that the Bible is a guide to life—I would have eagerly immersed myself in reading it, line by line, page by page, cover to cover, and back again. I would have relished the teachings and wisdom contained within it, getting to know the lessons so well that I could have saved myself from much trouble and confusion in my life.

You see, especially in my early years, if I had truly dedicated myself to reading and studying the Bible, I would have known the true nature and character of God. I would have known His Word, His plans, and His direction for me. I would have understood that obedience to Him leads me to make better choices.

Now that I embrace the Word of God as the truth upon which my character is developed and my life is defined, I recognize the importance of being obedient to God. It is through obedience that the true power of His Word comes alive and illuminates our lives, serving as a lamp to our feet and a light to our path (Psalm 119:105).

When we choose not to be obedient, we stumble around in the darkness of our lives, lacking purpose, direction, joy, and the capacity to experience the abundant life that God promises us through Jesus Christ. "I have come that they may have life, and that they may have it more abundantly" (John 10:10b).

In a state of disobedience and neglecting God's Word, we may find ourselves in less-than-desirable situations due to poor choices we have made. During those times, we may feel like we've hit rock bottom or that God has forsaken us. Far from it! It is at that point that God is ready and waiting for us to cry out to Him and say,
"Help! I can't do this anymore or go any further without You, Lord. Take me and guide me. I will follow Your will, not my own. I am ready to be obedient!"

Remember Mark, whom I mentioned several pages ago? Well, here's how my relationship with him finally ended:

I had reached a firm decision that I was done!

Done! Done! Done!

Finished! Over and done!
So I moved away from him and New York and returned to Florida. We still maintained our "business" relationship, and I convinced myself that we could continue to work together, even without being in a romantic relationship. However, God had a different plan in store for me.

One night after Bible study, a man approached me and said he needed to speak with me. Now, being wary of "strangers" or not, I was at church, so I felt obligated to be open to his conversation.

The conversation between the man and me went like this:

"Do you know me?" he asked.

"I have seen you before. You are Pastor Ricky's friend," I said.

"Yes, but you don't know me, right?"

"Right."

"I drove from Homestead to Cooper City—over an hour's drive—to give you a message from God. God said to tell you, 'The situation you are in, until you get out of it, you will be like a cripple in a wheelchair.'"

Of course, you must know that at this point, I was both laughing and crying hysterically. The man simply walked away, as if this were some kind of movie scene. Realizing that I was in the church parking lot with people around, I quickly composed myself. The awareness of my surroundings made me feel embarrassed because I didn't know who had witnessed the encounter between the man and me—and my strange and extreme reaction to our conversation.

Pastor Ricky approached me, and we were engaged in a brief chat when his phone rang. It was the man calling on the other end. He described me to Pastor Ricky and asked if I was still present.

Pastor Ricky handed me the phone.

"Did my message mean anything to you? Did it make sense?" the man asked.

"Yes."

"Good! Because I have no idea what it meant. I was just told to give you the message."

That was too much for me. I had never had an experience like that before. The funny thing is, for three months before the encounter with the man, God kept giving me messages that I needed to let go of the relationship with Mark, and I would say, "I hear You, Lord, but I am not ready yet."

God knows I am an in-your-face kind of girl, so He had to knock me over the head to get my full attention—because I can be so very stubborn.

Well, the very next day, I was home alone when the doorbell rang. I figured it was perhaps a package delivery because, in this age of cell phones, people (at least not the ones I know) don't just show up at your home unannounced—certainly not in Florida, where I lived in a gated community with 24-hour security.
"Good afternoon. I am here to pick up the blue Murano," he said.

"Pick it up? I didn't call the dealer; nothing is wrong with it! Why would you be picking it up?"

"I am here to repossess it."

114

"What? What do you mean?"

The man said gently, "I was asked to pick it up for non-payment."

I was so confused because missing a month's payment did not warrant repossession. This had to be a big mistake. Anyway, I gave the man the key and went back inside. I would handle it after he left. He was just doing his job, and I knew he couldn't help me.

The act of physically handing over the keys made reality sink in quickly. I closed the door, and the floodgates of emotion opened. I bawled my eyes out and cried incessantly. Losing the car was nothing compared to the fact that my house was also going into foreclosure because the mortgage wasn't being paid. Not paying a mortgage on a house in the United States is the surest way to ruin your credit.

Did I mention that the house was being occupied by Mark and not me? Now, I found myself jobless, without a car, and with jacked-up credit. When God wants to wake you up, He does so with life-altering stuff.

As I mentioned before, I can be extremely stubborn at times. I tend to dig my heels in and refuse to budge from a position. But God knows me very well. After all, He is my Father. He knows how to get my attention. He knew that I had to be pushed completely out of my comfort zone. He took away all my sense of control—albeit false.

Control was both my greatest strength and my greatest weakness. I loved being in control of my life and everything that impacted it, negatively or positively.

Well, it depends on how you define "reckless," right? Because some would say I had to have been reckless in my choices to end up in the position and situation I was in.

God left me no choice but to reach out to Him. He humbled me and made me completely dependent on Him. God knew that on my own, I could not endure the trials and afflictions that came my way—especially the magnitude and overwhelming frequency with which they arrived at that time. But He knew that through the power of Jesus Christ, I could endure all adversities and be strengthened.

God knew that I could do nothing in my own strength, but I could overcome anything in His strength and the power of His might. He knew that with faith and communion with Him through prayer and commitment to obedience to His will, I could endure and overcome even the most cruel and exhausting circumstances through Christ who strengthens me.

Therefore, I had to go into deep and earnest prayer and supplication to God, asking Him to help me overcome the challenges and deliver me from all "evil"—especially the ones I created. I put my trust and hope in Him. I depended totally on Him to see me through. I humbly submitted in obedience to His will and purpose for me.

By the grace of God, through Christ, I am happy to report that I came through the trials victoriously! My brother gifted me a car after mine was repossessed, and my best friend's sister bought my house that was up for foreclosure so that I would have a worry-free home. You will hear more about these two stories in greater detail in the next chapter.

The truth is, you can do anything through Christ who strengthens you. Without limitations, you can relax and be content in every state you are in—in adversity and prosperity, in poverty and plenty—and be able to bear all circumstances with contentment, knowing God "has your back" and will give you strength!

HOW DO I KNOW MY WORTH?

*I praise you because I am fearfully
and wonderfully made
Your works are wonderful, I know
that full well*
—Psalm 139:14

For many of us, especially Christians, the idea of loving ourselves is something we often shy away from or don't give much thought to.

We might be concerned that focusing on our value and self-worth could be seen as prideful or offensive to God. Alternatively, we may have been socialized from an early age not to think highly of ourselves, in an effort to remain humble. However, the truth is that whether we are aware of it or not, we all hold a perception of our value and worth. How we see ourselves greatly influences how we live our lives and relate to others.

The degree to which we recognize and appreciate our value also determines how we treat ourselves—with love, care, and respect. We can either think and speak negatively about ourselves, always looking for faults, or choose to be positive and affirming.

Our self-perception also affects the relationships we attract and sustain. If we believe we are unworthy or undeserving, we may find ourselves in unhealthy and dissatisfying relationships. Conversely, when we possess a strong sense of self-worth, we seek out mutually positive and empowering connections.

It all comes down to our sense of self-worth.

What is puzzling—especially among Christians—is that we readily accept we are made in the image and likeness of our Creator, whom we acknowledge and proclaim as great! Yet we struggle to accept the greatness within ourselves—we who are God's children.

We proudly affirm that we are fearfully and wonderfully made by God. Yet, the divine character within us, which calls us to embrace and express the beauty and wonder of who we are, often remains muted.

Only when we truly recognize and embrace the truth that we are inherently beautiful and special as God's children will we be open to accepting and expressing our greatness. With this affirmation, we can learn to love and honor ourselves—and others—as God intends.

God longs for us to live intentionally, making wise choices that support our well-being and keep us close to Him. He doesn't want us to place ourselves above everyone else, but He does desire that we become good stewards of ourselves. He wants us to choose behaviors and situations that align with our values.

But what if we struggle to believe we are valuable?

Hurtful relationships or traumatic experiences can make us feel inadequate. When we carry guilt, self-blame, and shame, we may feel tempted to hide or diminish our own worth and goodness.

The renowned leadership expert, speaker, and author John Maxwell often says, "Experience is not the best teacher." According to Maxwell, it is the evaluation and reflection on our experiences that bring true learning and insight. This insight shapes our attitudes and responses, determining our growth.

Therefore, we have a choice: we can allow fear, self-doubt, and anxiety to consume us in the wake of unpleasant or toxic experiences, or we can choose not to internalize negativity—and instead strive for better, claiming it for ourselves.

Allowing others to mistreat us or accepting poor treatment is not only unhealthy behavior; it also fails to align with the true concepts of love and humility—concepts that some may mistakenly believe are rooted in self-sacrifice at any cost. Such negativity dishonors the great worth and value bestowed upon us as God's creation.

The more we know and accept God's love for us, the more we will love ourselves. Likewise, the more we love ourselves, the deeper our understanding of God's love becomes.

As we embrace God's love, we must also extend that love inward—to ourselves. This enables us to be kind, forgiving, and patient with ourselves. It empowers us to treat ourselves and others in the way God does—with love.

Without self-love, we cannot truly love our neighbors. Only when we love ourselves can we genuinely give love to others.

Though it may not be easy, we must be intentional about choosing to love ourselves.

Once we understand, accept, and love ourselves, we reach a point where our self-worth no longer depends on people, accomplishments, or external factors. Our value comes from within, guided by God's view of who He created us to be.

As you reflect on the critical issue of knowing your worth, here are some questions to spend time asking yourself—and finding honest answers to:

How do I see myself?

Do I have a positive view of myself?

Do I focus on the good before the bad?

Take time to write down all the good things about yourself.

Do I recognize my accomplishments and their impact?

Do I take time to reflect on the great things I have done in my life and celebrate them?

Write down all the things you should have celebrated—and take the time to do so.

Do I undervalue my services?

If I am employed, am I delivering excellent service to my employer, who is my customer?

Am I being fairly compensated for the level of service I provide?

Is my level of service commensurate with my compensation?

You need to view yourself as a business, whether employed or self-employed.

Am I clear about what I stand for?

What am I not willing to settle for or compromise on?

What do I stand for?

Think about the wise adage: "If you don't stand for something, you will fall for anything."

Do I know what my true potential is?

Am I willing to put in the work to fulfill it?

What is my true potential?

What am I willing to do to accomplish it?

Am I willing to become the best version of myself?

How is my time spent?

Is it with people who are wasting my time?

Or am I wasting my time on useless activities that hold no value?

What am I spending my time on?

Do I spend time on activities that enhance my life and demonstrate that I understand the value—not only of who I am—but also how valuable my time is?

Whatever you invest your time, talents, and treasure in reveals where your heart truly lies and speaks to who you are.

I urge you, in consideration of loving yourself more, to take the following steps as a matter of great urgency and importance:
- Increase your self-understanding.
- Boost your self-acceptance.
- Recognize your self-worth.
- Take responsibility for yourself.
- Love yourself more!

Loving yourself more means valuing and respecting yourself as God's wonderful creation… fearfully and wonderfully made.

We are all a work in progress. The goal is to become better versions of ourselves each day.

STEP 4 - PURPOSE

LIVING WHO and WHOSE I AM

"For we are God's handiwork, created in Christ Jesus to do good works, which God prepared in advance for us to do."
Ephesians 2:10

We live in an age where the digital platform has become the stage for parading "virtual" images of ourselves and our lifestyles that have no basis in reality. Everything has become one big production aimed at creating the right impression and garnering "applause" and "likes." Notwithstanding the dictates of the age in which we live, I am a strong believer in authenticity and being true to ourselves, regardless of how we may be perceived.

We also live in an age where roles, rules, values, and attitudes have become a conundrum, making it increasingly challenging to navigate through life. However, I firmly believe that the quality of our lives is determined by the choices we make. Every choice carries outcomes and consequences. The question is, can we live with the consequences of our choices?

We have to hold ourselves accountable. I always caution that we should take the time and care to consider the consequences before we act. Sometimes, we become so entangled in confusion that we no longer seem to know or care about "which side is up"! Privacy has now become public, including our thoughts and body parts. Simple and mundane activities such as what we eat, what we wear, where we go, and who we are with are amplified and paraded for effect and crowd approval.

I was leading a discussion with a 12th-grade class in one of the monthly "Big Sister" sessions at my former high school. The discussion centered around an incident in which one of Jamaica's leading newspapers chose to feature images of young women posed in seemingly (or unseemly) notions of "indecency" on its front page.

One student made the point that the real issue was not about the moral conduct of the young ladies, as many critics of the pictures were quick to criticize, but rather the moral breach by the newspaper in publishing their pictures without permission.

In response, I presented the view that while the newspaper may have been morally wrong, they had the legal right to publish the pictures, with or without permission, because the images were already posted and published in the public space of social media by the young ladies. The newspaper had simply downloaded and republished them from that space.

I then further advised the students to be mindful of their "digital footprint"—whether it is a picture, comment, article, or anything else they post—as it is all fair game for anyone to use without their permission.

I challenged the students, as I challenge myself and encourage others to do the same, to take the time to explore the answers to these questions before leaping into action...
Can I live with how I represent myself today ten years from now?

If someone whose opinion I value were to examine my digital footprint, would it reflect positively or negatively on me?

Is my digital footprint aligned with my purpose, passion, and life plan?

Do my posts enable and empower others?

Does my way of being, in thoughts, words, and actions, truly reflect who I am and what I stand for?

I am still a work in progress.

I may not be where I want to be but thank God; I am not where I used to be.

I continue to grow daily on my journey of loving myself more.

Each day, I strive to live, express, and share with the world the beauty and power of that love.

I have two very close girlfriends in my life, both named Rochelle and nicknamed "RoRo" and "Rochy." To distinguish between them, I attach an affirming adjective that describes their energy to their nicknames.

They are both attorneys who are amazing powerhouses in their fields and exude positive energy. They are confident in who they are and embrace their greatness, which manifests itself in pure love that can only come from the light of God within them. Their energy lifts me and inspires me to unleash my greatness, and they motivate everyone around them to do the same.

When I walk in my greatness, I do so with confidence, pride, joy, and a deep sense of knowingness that I am walking in the image of my Creator.

In that heightened state of divine consciousness, I radiate light and attract light. I give and receive only the very best. It is during those moments that I am compelled to channel my inner "Adrenaline Roch" and triumphantly proclaim to the world, "I'm here! I didn't wake up this morning to be mediocre!"... or insignificant.

Thank God I have grown to truly know, appreciate, and accept myself.

Thank God I am awake and alive to the greatness of my God within me.

Thank God I am comfortable with the greatness of who I am.

Thank God I know what love is.

Thank God I am now able to claim that love and truly love myself.

Thank God that through the renewal of my mind and His grace, I now live, love, and let the greatness of God in me shine and illuminate the path for others to know, claim, and love themselves.

I claim the greatness of God in me and live in greatness. I am open to being a powerful channel of blessings to others, flowing from His greatness through me.

IRON SHARPENS IRON

"Iron sharpens iron, so one sharpens another."
—Proverbs 27:17

There was a time, as referenced in the Old Testament, when one iron blade was used to sharpen another blade until both became more effective tools. This common implementation of work or war provides a practical model for our human relationships.

According to The Bible Knowledge Commentary, "When iron is rubbed against another piece of iron, it shapes and sharpens it."

Similarly, people can help each other grow through their way of thinking, expressed in discussions, criticisms, suggestions, and ideas.

The proverb "Iron sharpens iron" reminds us of the value of being connected to people who are driven by the right motivation, vision, ambition, structure, wisdom, morals, and values—those who seek honorable and mutually beneficial relationships.

My father used to always repeat the well-worn adage: "Birds of a feather flock together."
Another familiar and frequently repeated saying he cautioned me with was: "Show me your company, and I'll tell you who you are."

When I was in high school, my father believed I was making poor choices and decisions, so one day he asked me to analyze my circle of friends. He asked, "Of all your friends, who do you think is most likely to get pregnant first?" Regrettably, my answer proved to be correct. That friend became pregnant before we finished high school.

My father wasn't being judgmental in his assessment of my friends; he simply paid attention to who they were. He observed their behavior, interests, and how their character was expressed.

His observations made him even more concerned about me—and rightfully so.

While most of my closest friends went off to Ivy League tertiary institutions, some even pursuing postgraduate degrees in highly regarded fields of study, I was left behind, having accomplished little at the time.

I had to play catch-up because I didn't make the right choices to grow in line with my abilities when I had the chance. So, while many of my peers surged ahead, I painfully trailed behind. Fortunately for me, I had a core group of positive friends who had been there since the beginning and stayed with me throughout life. They supported me through thick and thin, in sickness and sin.

These friends, even while pursuing their own growth and development, took the time to remind me of my potential for excellence and supported me as I rediscovered and unleashed that potential within.

There's a mutual benefit in the rubbing of two iron blades together—the edges become sharper, making the blades more efficient for cutting and slicing. We all need people who can help smooth out our rough edges and who genuinely have our best interests at heart.

At times, "sharpening" conversations, even from loving friends, may come across as harsh, mean, or judgmental. But it's important to recognize that they come from a place of care and a sincere desire to help us grow.

It is absolutely vital for each of us to build nurturing, growth-oriented relationships with the people in our lives. I once met a young lady in high school who became one of my closest friends—or so I thought. We later went to college together and grew even closer. But as time passed, I realized we didn't have as much in common as I'd believed, and her values were quite different from mine.

I discovered that she was judgmental and competitive. On many occasions, she tried to demean and undermine my character in front of others.

After deepening my relationship with God and gaining a clearer understanding of His plan for my life, I reached a point where I knew it was time to intentionally purge everything that wasn't positive, uplifting, or beneficial to my walk with God. That included relationships.

That "friend" had to go.
I took time to carefully evaluate the people I attracted and allowed into my life, choosing instead to focus on building and maintaining high-quality relationships.

I came to appreciate the value of building godly, growth-centered relationships—relationships with people whose conversations, discussions, and actions are empowering, enabling, and lead me closer to God and to personal growth.

This isn't about distancing oneself from people in general. It's about following God's command to love and care for all people without judgment, while also choosing to build close personal connections with those who share similar values and faith—just as Jesus did.

It's about managing boundaries in our lives and understanding that those we allow into our inner circle should be different from casual acquaintances whose influence may not be positive or meaningful.

A key part of developing deep, personal relationships is recognizing that they should never be one-sided. Both individuals should desire the best for each other.

People who bring negativity or provoke toxic dynamics—those who don't nurture love, peace, and harmony—only distract and subtract from our lives. In contrast, God-honoring relationships help both parties grow and experience the fullness of life that God promises.

As I reflect on my formative years up to now, I realize that the quality of my family and friend relationships has had a significant influence on my life. There were moments when their counsel and guidance helped me make necessary changes in my approach to life.

Engaging in meaningful conversations with close family and trusted friends has often expanded my thinking in ways I could not have managed on my own. This form of "sharpening" may well be the most valuable.

Even my deeply rooted Christian beliefs and worldview have been strengthened and refined through heartfelt conversations with trusted people who, like me, seek a deeper understanding of God's ways and the realities of life.

Spiritual and mental sharpness comes from being in the company of good people. We help one another become sharper. I am immensely grateful for my strong, powerful, and diverse village of family and friends.

SHARPENERS and SHARPENING

The Word of God states that we are to sharpen one another in times of meeting, fellowship, or any other interaction. The Scriptures emphasize the importance of building close relationships with quality people who help improve us.

We need close relationships with people we trust and respect—people who can examine our lives, identify areas of weakness and challenge, and work with us to address those areas. These individuals, with whom we share a close and significant personal bond, are not critical or negative people who take pleasure in pointing out faults or flaws. Instead, they help keep us accountable and contribute to our growth through positive and constructive conversations. They help us recognize our amazing qualities despite our shortcomings and inspire us to strive for more—to be more and to do more.

The act of "sharpening" is fueled by a heartfelt desire to assist, and in the process, lovingly and graciously provide input that leads to personal improvement and life-changing strategies.

God has truly blessed me with exceptional individuals who serve as sharpeners in my life. Together, we mutually benefit from each other's presence. At different times, each person has been used by God to help the other—as both pieces of iron work together to achieve the desired purpose: to sharpen each other.

The simple proverb "Iron sharpens iron" illustrates that God expects us to live and serve in community, positively enabling and empowering one another. He desires that we build loving and growing relationships with each other.

This community of individuals with whom I have cultivated loving and growing relationships represents different areas and phases of my life. I greatly value family—both biological and "found" families. They are precious and irreplaceable to me. I cherish them all—my biological parents, adopted parents, siblings, other relatives, and in-laws—as well as my spiritual family. They are my rocks.

I have foundational friends from early childhood, elementary school, tertiary education, and professional life. Some are fantastic, dependable, and uplifting friends; others serve as mentors. I hold all of them dear. These are the individuals I allow to speak into my life and influence me because I know, ultimately, they have my best interests at heart.

Yes, we can learn from anyone, but we need God-guided wisdom and discernment to know whom to trust with our personal matters and from whom to seek counsel.

I am especially thankful for the gift of my family. My parents, siblings, and relatives have all been—and continue to be—the iron to my iron.

I have been blessed with a phenomenal mother who inspires, supports, and serves as a role model in my life. She exemplifies what it means to walk in love and demonstrates unconditional love. The blessings she has been to others have multiplied and returned to me manifold. She taught me the importance and value of independence while also instilling the virtues of a Proverbs 31 woman: "of noble character" and "worth far more than rubies." She has been a strong tower of support and my biggest cheerleader. My mother has brought tremendous meaning and value to my life, and I attribute much of the best in me to her.

My father is a philosopher—a wise sage—an unflappable and rational sounding board who dispenses sound advice, practical guidance, and unwavering support. I love him dearly and thank God for the role he has played in sharpening me. God bless him.

Thinking about my siblings brings tears to my eyes. They are some of the most important people in my life. Their children, spouses, and the added gifts of in-laws bring immense joy and blessings to my world. I truly hit the jackpot with all of them in my life!

My siblings motivate and inspire me, holding me accountable in all areas of life. I could write an entire book on my deep love and affection for them. From my scholarly, bright spark of a Ph.D. brother to my equally brilliant baby brother, and my amazing sister who is a loving wife, incredible mother, and a creative powerhouse—I celebrate them all and cherish the sharpening effect they have on my life.

My aunts and second mothers—Faith, Angela, Jen, and Mama H—encourage, correct, guide, and support me through the various phases and seasons of life. Their stories and journey with me could fill several books. I am incredibly blessed to have them.

My amazing village of family and friends—both individually and collectively—has had a powerful and positive impact on my life. I have a friend who shows up with a camera in hand whenever I have a formal speaking engagement. She pushes me forward and upward in ways that may be annoying at times but for which I am always grateful. She encouraged me to write this book and has been one of my biggest and most enduring supports. Thank you, CD.

I have another girlfriend who constantly celebrates me because that's who she is. She gives everyone in her inner circle a nickname or alias—like HP (Hawaiian Princess) or CG ("the spiritual sensei"—which is me, LOL). She even bought me a mug that says "Spiritual Gangster." She is also my business partner, and I am constantly in awe of her brilliance and her capacity to love.

When I decided to pursue my Master's in Business Administration (MBA), the journey was far from easy. Having been out of school for so long, it required a major readjustment to academic rigor. Additionally, academics do not come naturally to me.

At that time, a young lady I considered my little sister walked beside me through it all. Along the way, we gained good company and support from two others, who remain part of my inner circle to this day.

We held each other accountable throughout the program, leveraging each other's strengths and lifting each other beyond our weaknesses.

One of us ensured we were always punctual. Another made sure no assignment was ever missed. Yet another worked tirelessly to ensure we were prepared for exams and submitted top-quality papers.

We were an amazing team—and even better friends. It's a beautiful thing when friends expect excellence; we, in turn, begin to expect it of ourselves and support one another in reaching it.

I have friends I call when I need words of comfort or encouragement. They are gentle with me and share their truth with honesty and integrity, without making me feel wrong or diminished. They correct me with love and hold me accountable.

Then there are two other friends who are incisive and brutally honest in delivering their truths. They are my go-to sounding boards who never fail to give me a reality check.

They know me well—sometimes better than I know myself. They even have the audacity (and uncanny accuracy) to anticipate my unspoken thoughts or decisions and veto them in favor of their own suggestions. Yet they embody the truth that God never points out weaknesses without providing solutions.

Whenever good friends sincerely want to help us grow and truly desire what is best for us, we must accept their counsel, advice, or constructive criticism with a willing and open heart.

I have my ride-or-die friend who understands me when I just need to be or do nothing. I call her my wife. We can spontaneously decide to go to the beach, countryside, or anywhere at all—no long-winded planning or deliberation necessary. There is no "static" between us.

Then I have my big sister/friend who is absolutely invaluable when it comes to negotiation and business. She's the master at managing our rather strong-willed mothers and our "once upon a time" out-of-order younger brothers. We are deeply familiar with each other's journeys and share a profound understanding.

There are friends who take charge and declare, "We're doing our vision boards on this day, at this time, and here's what you need to bring!" or "We're having Sunday dinner this week because we need family time!" Their loving, get-up-and-go, can-do spirit energizes me and gets things moving.

I have my ray-of-sunshine friend, Rochelle, who is an amazing burst of positive energy. She radiates joy and happiness—and happens to be an actual happiness coach.

Conversely, I have a particular pain-in-the-butt friend who sometimes seems to take more from me than he gives. But even in that, he has toughened me and taught me to be firm—especially in business. Through him, I've learned to recognize and honor my own worth and value.

I have my mentors—people who inspire me to unleash the greatness within. They possess maturity, generosity of spirit, and genuine care. They offer a listening ear, a hand to hold, a shoulder to lean on, a brain to pick, and so much more. I can interact with them comfortably and confidentially. Some are my parents' friends, and others are the children of those friends with whom I grew up. My pastor is also one of my mentors. I bounce everything off him. I'm so grateful for his accessibility and guidance. He truly is a shepherd.

Of course, I have my prayer warriors. These are individuals who know, trust, serve, and obey the same God I do. They don't think I'm crazy when I talk about God speaking to me or doing miraculous and incredible things in my life. For all these reasons and more, I deeply value my prayer warriors—whose prayers sharpen me.

Then there are the people whom God places in our lives seemingly out of nowhere. We marvel at the unlikely circumstances surrounding our meeting and the sudden fusion of energies. Often, out of these "strange" unions, amazing outcomes emerge—exactly what we needed in that moment or season of our lives. My husband was one of those unlikely occurrences.

The concept of iron sharpening iron obviously implies the presence of at least two pieces of iron. One tool cannot become sharper without the help of another. Left alone, both blades would remain dull and ineffective. That's why it's so essential that we attract and maintain relationships with individuals who will sharpen the iron in us—just as we, in turn, sharpen the iron in them.

Good friends can sharpen us. Family can sharpen us. Anyone who speaks God's empowering truth and love into our lives without reservation can sharpen us.

2 Timothy 3:16–17 confirms this truth:

"All Scripture is inspired by God and profitable for teaching, for reproof, for correction, for training in righteousness; so that the man of God may be adequate, equipped for every good work."

Therefore, we must strive to build, maintain, and treasure positive, growing relationships with others who can strengthen our walk with God—the One who guides and directs our paths.

When we live in positive relationships with one another and help each other improve our effectiveness as children of God, we are, in fact, sharpening—and being sharpened by—each other.

STEP 5: LEADERSHIP
LEAD WITH LOVE

DOMINION

Then God said,
"Let us make mankind in our image, in
our likeness,
So that they may rule over the fish in the
sea and the birds in the sky,
Over the livestock and all the wild
animals,
And over all the creatures that move
along the ground."
So God created mankind in his own
image,
In the image of God he created them;
Male and female he created them.
—Genesis 1:26-27

I remind myself every day that I am a child of the King, created in His image and likeness. When I think of God and words to describe Him, I think of: great, awesome, powerful, amazing, marvelous, beautiful, bountiful, benevolent, loving, caring, compassionate, faithful, forgiving, comforting, empowering, just, true, holy, and so much more.

Knowing that we are created in the image and likeness of God makes us worthy and deserving to describe ourselves with those words too.

He is the Creator, Ruler, and Master of all the heavens and the earth. He has given me dominion over every living thing that moves upon the earth.

It is important to note and remember, however, that dominion is spiritual. It is not arbitrary rulership. It is not about commanding and demanding at will. It comes with effort, responsibility, and partnership with God.

To have dominion is to rule, be in charge, and have the ability to request or command—and expect the fulfillment of that appeal.
I have the ability to rule and master, not with arrogance but with humility and love. And above all, with mindfulness of God's way, will, and purpose.

Notice I said we have the ability—for it is God who makes us able. It is God who enables us to live in dominion with love, care, respect, and nurturing of our physical and social environments, and in harmony with each other. Dominion is spiritual, and it falls under the auspices of God. It is only effective and effectual when it submits totally to the will of God.

Jesus Christ is a model of how to live in dominion. He stood steadfast and immovable in the worship and work of God as a servant leader. He conquered self and stood in control and authority. His total worship of and commitment to God enabled Him to stand in authority.

As a servant leader, Jesus led by example and taught us—through His own life practices—that spiritual dominion begins inside of us. We will never be able to exercise power or authority over anything until we, like Christ, have brought our minds, bodies, and spirits under subjection to the will of God. Jesus was able to do anything and everything He was purposed to do by the will of the Lord. He taught us by His lived example that whatever mountain may be in front of us and in our way, we can take dominion over it. We don't have to be intimidated by it or let it stand in our way. We don't have to let that mountain keep us from our place of power and dominion in God.

I recall when I started a new job. I had been there for about six months, and my team was responsible for building out an entire division from scratch—starting from the ground up. Prior to this job, I had received eight other job offers, all at an executive leadership level. I didn't apply for any of these jobs.

Dominion is about operating in excellence at all times because that's just the nature and character of who you are created to be. Always give your best, regardless of who is watching. The fact that I gave my best in a key leadership position with a top-tier multinational company operating in the Caribbean and Latin American market enabled me, after leaving, to attract and receive nine more executive-level job offers from other organizations—even though I had not applied for any of them.

I thought I was being sought after because I had earned the hard-won reputation of bringing value to organizations, including the one in which I was then working.

One day, however, I was at work, and the owner of the company said to me, "You have been here for six months, and I don't know what purpose you serve! I have wasted my money because I don't know what you have done for six months—nothing!"

I was absolutely flummoxed! Somehow, I managed to scrape up my badly bruised ego and mortally wounded pride from the floor, went home, and bawled my eyes out.

I started to doubt myself and wonder if I could do the job. Was I mistaken in believing that I had any ability whatsoever? Was I wrong in thinking that others saw me as having outstanding capabilities?

The feelings of doubt, insecurity, inadequacy, failure, and shame had by now invaded my territory and become clamorous noises in my head and a leaden weight in my spirit.

I had to summon every ounce of willpower to rise from that desperate and desolate space and reach up to the higher authority of God—affirming my kinship with Him, His greatness within me, and His purpose for me.

My spirit rose in affirmation of my value, worth, and impact—regardless of the criticism. I was reminded that I am created to have dominion, to own and command my space, in spite of adverse distractions. I affirmed the truth that "I can do all things through Christ who strengthens me."

In that organization, in the role for which I was hired, I knew I had put in the work to lead effectively and achieve successful outcomes. After all, building something great from nothing in six months was an unreasonable request.

I was confident and assured in what I was doing. I was focused and diligent in executing what I knew needed to be done.

On top of that, I knew I was led there for a reason. I trusted God to place me where He wanted me to be.

At first, my mind screamed, "Leave the job!" But the still, small voice within me said, "Stay put! This too shall pass."

I chose to yield to His will. I submitted myself in prayerful appeal to God for His divine intervention—enabling me to renew my mind and spirit, and be strengthened in my humble resolve to stay the course and remain in the organization.

Surrendering to the still, small voice, I blocked out all negativity and remained on the job, continuing to be as creative, productive, focused, disciplined, and diligent as I have always been—despite the scathing criticism of my professional performance. I knew what needed to be done, and I stayed focused and executed.

Two months later, the same owner of the business told me he was sorry for his vitriolic outburst. He said that upon closely assessing my performance, he realized I was the best hiring decision he had ever made and that I was doing a great job! He apologized.

Imagine that—if only you knew the ego of a Jamaican.

Having a kingdom mindset is critical. We must think and operate as leaders—specifically as servant leaders. If we want to be transformational, as all servant leaders must be, we can't focus solely on ourselves or operate within the confines of our narrow self-interest. We must be generous, compassionate, and inclusive of others.

If you own a house and don't maintain or care for it, it will start to fall apart. The same is true for our lives, families, churches, businesses, communities, country, and the world. We must always be mindful of how the decisions we make impact not only our own lives but also the lives of others and everything else that is a part of our world.

We have to choose to be different. We must first take dominion over ourselves—our habits, desires, and unbridled indulgences that do not serve or satisfy our well-being. Only then can we expect to have dominion over anything else.

Dominion is knowing who we are in Christ and understanding that we can do what God says we can do, have what God says we can have, and be who God says we can be.

Many things in life will scare us, whether due to uncertainty, insecurity, or other sources of fear. But stepping boldly forward—despite fear—demonstrates dominion. People who take dominion are leaders. Leaders learn through their tests and trials. They grow through their experiences, and they trust God.

In March 2020, I was laid off. It was the first time I had lost a job—and it happened at the beginning of a pandemic. I was very clear and certain about what I no longer wanted to do, but I was quite hazy about where I was going or what I was supposed to do next. I knew I did not want to work in corporate anymore, so even though I lost my job, I was at peace.

I have never been one to worry about money or how I would live because God has always taken care of that. I wasn't really worried. In fact, I was somewhat excited! That excitement was solidified when my business partners celebrated when I lost my job! LOL.

So while I wasn't worried about being out of work, I was a little unsure of my footing as I moved forward. Upon close examination, I found that in some areas of my life, I was bold and unwavering in exercising the power of real dominion—but in far too many other areas, I was weak and wavering.

Thankfully, I had already established my own businesses a year before my untimely disengagement from my job and before the onset of the pandemic. The businesses are REDEFINE Business Services Limited and Ready to Emerge Limited.

As I struggled to figure out what was next—without the support of a corporation behind me—it dawned on me, upon reflection, how easy it had been for me to walk seemingly in dominion with purposeful and confident strides when I was leading and serving in someone else's organization and not my own. I was bold and confident, full of vim, vigor, and vitality when I was minding someone else's business—but faltering and hesitant when it came to minding my own.

I thought perhaps the confidence I had placed in the power of a multinational brand had supported and enabled my success in building a powerful local brand. But now, on my own, without the shelter and security of a big brand behind me, I felt uncertain about my abilities.

Now I only had myself. I had to put myself out there and become my own big brand. The prospect was daunting, and I didn't feel equal to the task.

As a child of God, it seemed I had not fully understood—or perhaps had forgotten—that my Father had gifted me with the power of dominion as my birthright.

I quickly realized that a lack of understanding and a failure to live in dominion could have spiritual consequences and diminish my relationship with God.

As I progressed with my business and continued my journey with God, I became more deeply aware of how crucial it is to claim and live in dominion in my walk with Him.

God wants us to have dominion in all areas of our lives—spiritually, financially, in relationships, careers, health, well-being, and every other aspect. In partnership with Him, we are called to be bold and exercise power, authority, and control.

God within me is my big brand—my very own multinational conglomerate of all that is great, positive, prosperous, and impactful.

With God as my big brand, I am empowered to live and operate effectively and successfully in dominion—in harmony with myself and others, and according to God's will and purpose for my life.

Living in dominion is about claiming purpose, walking in purpose, and staying on course with purpose. It is knowing that you were created for a purpose—and to live in that purpose.

Living in dominion also means living mindfully and making intentional choices. It is choosing between ego and spirit. It is choosing to focus on what really matters—love.

I used to be easily distracted and taken off course from my purpose by responding to requests from others. My ego led me to say yes "because I could" and because I was capable. I didn't want to disappoint anyone or risk a task not being executed well if I didn't do it. However, doing things just because I could—rather than because I truly wanted to, or because it was actually important to me—distracted me from my purpose and left me feeling dissatisfied. It left my spirit diminished and misaligned with greatness.

I wanted to spend time with the right people, enjoying unhurried moments or creating and enabling the realization of possibilities. I wanted to be free and open, unhindered by demands on my time and resources that were not aligned with my purpose. I wanted to respond fully and without reservation, building a stronger relationship with my Creator, answering only to His call on my life, and serving Him in spirit and in truth—always trusting and obeying. I wanted, by His grace, to love, honor, and empower others without restraint. I wanted to love myself more—without hesitation.

I learned the hard way that saying yes to everyone sometimes meant diminishing my ability to execute with excellence. That cost me reputational embarrassment and strained some good relationships.

Now, I can declare:

I live in dominion of my life, through the transformation of the Holy Spirit. I continually strive to be free from fear, clutter, and all that does not serve me well. Accountability matters. I am a continuous work in progress.

I live in abundance through God's good grace and provision!

I live in greatness, for He has made me so!

I live in love—for myself and for others—for that is all there is.
I live and revel in a transformed life.

Like me, you too can live a transformed life.

I invite you to ponder these questions, go into deep reflection, and answer honestly:

Are you living in dominion?

If not, why not?

Do you want to live in dominion?

If yes, why?

How do you want to be transformed?

What steps do you need to take to make it happen?

Who can you ask to help you on your journey?

STEP 6: EXECUTE

BLOOM WHERE YOU ARE PLANTED

To bloom is to grow with the grace of God within us, causing us to be loving, gracious, patient, and kind to those around us.

When we bloom with God's grace, we flourish with love. We share what we have with others. We are humble and forgiving, and we do not harbor anger, resentment, and bitterness against anyone, regardless of their attitudes and behaviors.

Blooming where we are planted means to flourish despite challenging circumstances. It means flourishing in faith, knowing and trusting that God is with us in every moment and any situation.

It is about seeing and claiming God's blessings, even when the flourishing doesn't always look like what we expect with riches, favors, and accolades.

God is the one who plants us, and while I'll be the first to admit that I sometimes question God's timing, I have to remind myself that I can't see the "end game" like He can. He is far wiser and more knowledgeable than I am.

So trusting Him means surrendering my will to His. It is in this surrender that I can be obedient. It is through obedience that I can bloom where I am planted.

No one blooms overnight, however. Blooming is a process. It is often a struggle. But by God's good grace, under His nurture and care, and through our obedience to His will and purpose for our lives, we will bloom and flourish in an abundance of blessings.

You see, a major step in learning how to bloom where God plants us is to grow where we are planted. A seed doesn't become a flower overnight. It takes time, water, sun, and nutrients before any blooming occurs.

Despite how alluring the stories of overnight success and their often accompanying stories of great wealth, accolades, and comfort are, they are very often just that—stories with no basis in reality.

We must be willing to grow with God's truth and God's Word.

Bloom where you are planted. In every opportunity you are given, be your best and give your best! In the same way that seeds are planted, we are also planted. Sometimes, we find ourselves in seemingly perfect spots that are great for blooming. Other times, we are planted in what appear to be seriously inhospitable spots that could hinder growth and blooming. There are even times when we choose to transplant ourselves from where we were originally planted, and those are the times we must pay attention to the lessons. Growth often comes from discomfort.

The truth, however, is that we cannot plant ourselves. Only God can plant us. We may not have a choice in where we are planted, but we should accept without hesitation and be confident that wherever God plants us, He will enable us to bloom.

I will be the first to admit, though, that while I accept that it is God who plants us, there are times when I don't understand His timing and His purpose. During those times, I have to remind myself that I need to trust Him and surrender my will to Him. After all, He works all things together for my good.

The story is often told, in varying ways, through different experiences, of a flower growing and blooming through a crack in a concrete surface (the road or otherwise). The plant would often be used as a symbol of acceptance, determination, and resilience.

I recall here, for your interest and reflection, the abridged version of one such story of the blooming plant and what the occurrence meant to the author, Peter Lundell.

The story goes as follows:

> A weed grows at the end of my driveway where it crosses the sidewalk into the street. One day it sprouted white flowers. It is small . . . But it's beautiful.
>
> It is completely surrounded and wedged in by slabs of concrete . . . So it grows anyway in the little dirt it finds between the slabs and with the little water spared by the arid sky.
>
> Do you ever feel like this flower, small yet proudly beautiful?
>
> Resilient yet vulnerable?
>
> Stubbornly doing your thing, yet not sure about the future?

They say bloom where you're planted. So, best to get on with it—even if you feel as if your life is wedged in by concrete. Even if you're small. Even if you go unnoticed.

A flower like this won't last forever. None of us will. So bloom as well as you can with what you've got, right here and right now.

A flower like this will do best if it's transplanted into a pretty pot with good soil. If the chance comes, take it.

If not, remember that God gives the sun and the occasional rain no matter where we're planted.

So bloom even in the cracks. And do it boldly and beautifully.

I thank Peter Lundell for sharing that story and his profound insights with us in his online CONNECTIONS post at PeterLundell.com

Regardless of your environment or the people around you, you can bloom.

When I think of blooming, I think of growth. For a flower to bloom, it must first grow. Its roots must be firmly grounded, and it needs nurturing—water, sunlight, the right environment, and care.

You may feel stuck in a place where you're being mistreated or not nurtured, but consider what you can learn and how you can grow through it.

Many of us make choices that are less than ideal. We find ourselves in situations that could have been avoided if we had made better decisions. The beautiful thing is, no matter how poor our choices have been, God always finds a way to work them out for our good—if we ask Him and allow Him into our situations.

Blooming where we are planted means always giving our best and learning as much as we can within and through the experiences we encounter. It means ensuring that we are growing and becoming better through the process.

If you're in a job you don't love, remind yourself why you're there, and think about what you can gain from the experience. How can you become better?

If it's a difficult relationship—or one that wasn't right for you—think about what you've learned, even if it's simply what not to do. How has it helped shape or strengthen you?

If you're in a new environment—especially if you're an introvert—consider what you have to gain from stepping outside your comfort zone.

If it's a new position, try not to overwhelm yourself by overthinking. Take one step at a time, treat others the way you want to be treated, and spend time learning and observing before you begin implementing.

Loving myself more means living in surrender to God's will. It means accepting where I am planted and choosing to bloom with excellence. That little flower is me, you, each of us—growing and blooming despite our circumstances or environments. Every one of us can bloom in the place where God has allowed us, according to His will and purpose for our lives, if we allow Him to mold us.

Ask yourself these questions and give thoughtful consideration to your answers:

Do you live the truth of growing where you are planted?

Are you accepting of wherever you may be planted at this moment?

Are you doing and giving your best wherever you are planted?

Are you willing to submit in humble surrender to God's will and grow regardless of the conditions or circumstances you are in?

Remind yourself of the challenges you've grown through. Are you ready for another stage to bloom?

Are you blooming in excellence?

LIVE AND WORK WITH EXCELLENCE

Whatever you do, work at it with all your heart,
as working for the Lord, not for human masters.
—Colossians 3:23

I believe that every experience in life is a learning opportunity, and it's all a part of God's plan to mold and shape us according to His will and purpose for our lives.

I believe we are always meant to grow and learn.

I believe we are called to walk in authority, knowing that we were placed here for a reason and purpose, and to live and walk in that purpose.

I believe that some paths we take, even when we don't know how or why we ended up there, provide us with the hindsight to see God's hand in everything.

From my own wayward life, filled with seemingly poor choices and decisions, I can see how God turned what could have been for ill into good. I can see how He turned my "ashes into beauty" and created powerful testimonies for His honor and glory.

Through it all, I am pleased to report that, by the grace of God, I have many testimonies of His greatness and goodness. Indeed, my entire life is a testament to the fact that God qualifies the called. So much of what I thought I wasn't ready for, qualified to do, or otherwise unprepared for, God made possible.

Earlier, I shared how, inexplicably, out of the blue, I was offered a job in marketing (for which I had not applied) to work for a huge multinational corporation in Jamaica.

I was asked to submit my resume if I was interested in the offer. At first, I hesitated to do so because, in my mind, I wasn't qualified. I knew nothing about being a brand manager, had no formal training in marketing, and had never worked in a corporate setting. After all, my degree was in sociology/anthropology.

But as I thought about it some more, I realized that God had been preparing me for that opportunity.

You see, without realizing it, I had amassed over twelve years of experience working for Jamaica's leading model agency and entertainment company at the time. I learned most of what I knew in logistics, management, marketing, and many other valuable professional and personal skills from the CEO of that business. In fact, many of the skills and abilities I have since developed, and the successes I enjoy today as a professional, can be traced back to his tutelage and mentorship, which began when I was about 15 years old. And yes, a significant portion of my professional experience and expertise was gained through working with his organization.

Later, I worked as a marketing, public relations, and events coordinator with a clothing company, where, again, without prior formal training for the job, I was selected for the position and gained considerable knowledge and expertise over time.

So, you see, contrary to what I had initially thought when contemplating the job offer from the multinational corporation, I was well-equipped and a good fit for the job.

Sometimes, many of us are given opportunities, and we allow our fears and self-doubt to derail us or create a default future for ourselves. We either do not take up these opportunities or, if we do, we do not always optimize them.

Some people, on the other hand, will seize opportunities, even if they are not ready. If it's a job opportunity, they will apply, sometimes get the job, and then figure out afterward how to do the job.

It's all about our mindsets, which inform our choices, attitudes, and behavior.

I remember some time ago, I received a call from a gentleman I had never met before. I knew who he was because we had close friends in common, but we had never met.

He called me, in Florida, to inform me that his brand manager was going on maternity leave for three months. He needed a replacement, and several people had recommended me to him.

The offer provided me with the opportunity to work as the interim brand manager on a contract basis, initially for three months, until the brand manager returned from maternity leave.

That part of the story provides an excellent example of the choices we make regarding whom we let into our lives and how we accommodate people. It also emphasizes the need to cultivate a spirit of goodwill for all. As I said, I hadn't lived in Jamaica for over twelve years, yet several people recommended me for the job.

Treating all individuals with love, care, and respect, regardless of who they are or how we encounter them, is to express the will of God in action: "Love your neighbor as yourself." Therefore, we must always intentionally and unconditionally strive to maintain positive relationships with all people. You never know when you may need to serve one another.

I have worked in many different industries and held various roles, but I have consistently given my best in all of them. In every job I've ever had—whether at a model agency, clothing company, law firm, ice company, leading manufacturing and distribution outfit, multinational corporation, or non-profit organization—I have always given my best. I strive to achieve excellence.

From being early or on time, being prepared to serve and lead, empowering and building the capacity of others to achieve excellence, ongoing investment in my growth and development, learning from lessons, adopting a growth mindset, and much more... I did it all with a spirit of excellence.

All the aforementioned examples and more indicate my absolute focus and dedication to operating in excellence, which, for me, means giving my best.

The total of my best may not always reach the 100 mark required. Sometimes my best may amount to only 50, 40, or less, or perhaps up to 80 or more. But it is my best, and my excellence is expressed through it.

God requires me, and all of us, to be excellent, for we are born with His spirit of excellence within us. As His child, I work in humble obedience to His will and strive to undertake all my tasks with His spirit of excellence.

I once met a young lady who shared comments with me about her job and the portfolio she managed. She said, "I have asked the company to send me for training, and they always send someone else!"

Upon hearing her remarks, my immediate thought was that she had gotten it twisted! She should not be waiting for others to invest in her growth. She should live and work with such a spirit of excellence that would lead her to invest in her own development, regardless of whether or not the company is ready or willing to invest in her.

God has created and equipped us with the tools to unleash and fully express our excellence. He has given each of us unique skills, interests, and abilities. Moreover, He has placed us in our circumstances to exercise dominion over the earth and all situations by His power and for His glory.

So, when the tiny seed from which the little plant sprouted found itself between the dark, rough, and tough cracks of concrete, instead of withering away and eventually perishing in despair, it settled in and strived mightily to make the best of the situation and be excellent—regardless!

Furthermore, the seed, having sprouted against all odds, did not indulge in daydreaming or waste valuable productive time thinking about a different life, a different situation, being in a better spot, or even a new community. It solely focused its energy on growing, utilizing to the maximum capacity whatever nurturing resources of earth, moisture, or sunlight came its way, and steadfastly moved toward blooming!

That is excellence!

It is the Spirit of God within us that enables us to live, grow, and bloom according to the stages of our lives, regardless of where we may be planted and the conditions that affect our growth and development.

Consider these questions and thoughtfully respond:

Do you believe you are born to live and express excellence?

What does excellence mean for you in health and wellbeing, intimate relationships, friendships, socializing, fun and recreation, career/business, finances, spiritual and physical environment, personal growth, and other areas?

Are you living in excellence?

Are you a living example of God's excellence in you?

Are you satisfied with your expression of excellence?

Excellence is one of the purposes and joys of the life God created us to live and fulfill. Committing to excellence is not only a powerful life choice, but within that power lies all the greatness of who God created us to be.

What is holding you back? Why?

Unleash the power of excellence within you in every way, in every situation, in every moment, every day!

We should always strive to be excellent because God is excellence, and all His ways are excellent.
When we live and work in excellence, we honor God. He has provided us with opportunities and given us the ability to fulfill our tasks.

This commitment to excellence as a way of being has opened up so many doors of amazing opportunities and invaluable experiences for me. The excellence I express is reciprocated by the excellent results I achieve and the immense satisfaction I receive.

I am compelled to express my excellence and impelled by the Holy Spirit to be excellent, even if no one notices and applauds. Like the little plant that bloomed between the cracks, few people may have noticed it, and some may even trample it, but it bloomed anyway. It is in its nature to do so.

As the great Greek philosopher Aristotle reportedly said, "We are what we repeatedly do. Excellence is not an act, but a habit." It's okay if you mess up; we all do. Don't let that derail or control you. Dust off and try to make it happen again.

And as the Bible says, "Whatever you do, work heartily, as for the Lord and not for men" (Colossians 3:23 ESV).

"Finally, brothers, whatever is true, whatever is honorable, whatever is just, whatever is pure, whatever is lovely, whatever is commendable, if there is any excellence, if there is anything worthy of praise, think about these things" (Philippians 4:8 ESV).

BE EXPECTANT

MAKE ROOM FOR SOMETHING NEW

See I am doing a new thing! Now it springs up; do you not perceive it? I am making a way in the wilderness and stream in the wasteland.

- Isaiah 43:19

I t took me about four years to write this book. While much of it had already been completed and had gone through two publishers, I knew something was missing. I just didn't know what it was.

It's important to reiterate that self-love is a continuous journey. There will be times when we make choices that don't align with our values or don't reflect our growth. However, those are the moments when we need to show ourselves grace.

After leaving what I thought was a healthy three-year relationship—one built on mutual care and consideration—I realized that we were still unequally yoked in several ways: spiritually, culturally, and in terms of our priorities. Although we had no major issues, there came a time when I realized we were moving in different directions, so it was time to part ways. It was a mature and amicable separation, which also marked my growth and my ability to make better choices.

In November 2021, my church was doing a fast, and if I'm completely honest, I had fasted before, but this time felt different. God told me it was time to truly consecrate myself, to dig deep, and to spend quality time with Him—time to listen, instead of constantly doing.

I wasn't in a great place for about a year and a half before that. As I mentioned earlier, in 2020, when COVID-19 hit, I lost my job. While it was actually a blessing, as I didn't want to be there, the timing was unsettling, as anyone could imagine. I was fortunate to have a support system that encouraged me and even celebrated the loss of my steady income in US dollars—which means a lot in Jamaica! They helped me maintain a positive mindset, reminding me that losing my job was actually a good thing because God had a plan, and it was time for me to execute it.

For the first four months, Jamaica was on complete lockdown. At that time, I lived by myself. I was used to always being busy, engaging with others, and having a lot to do. Now, I found myself having to be still, alone with my thoughts and without any physical interaction. I was going crazy! It impacted me so much that I started counseling. The truth is, it was long overdue. Through therapy, I uncovered so much that, for the first six weeks, I cried and cried. Then I had to take a break from counseling. I'm not generally an emotional person, so dealing with emotions for six weeks was overwhelming. As you know, emotional and mental exhaustion is the worst kind. I'm used to compartmentalizing; I do that well. I put things in a box and lock them away because, for me, processing emotions seemed like an unnecessary waste of time.

A couple of months later, restrictions eased, and we were able to travel. I was accustomed to seeing my family at least once a month, but it had been almost a year since I could visit them. So, as soon as travel was permitted, I hopped on the first flight out. I decided to spend most of my time in Florida, as by then, I was consulting and could work from anywhere. I had some projects I was working on, but the reality was that they weren't paying me on time. As a result, I found myself living off savings and incurring debt that I was struggling to pay.

I felt like I was drowning—not because of my finances, but because my life was spiraling in a direction I wasn't comfortable with. I wasn't happy with my professional situation. Let me explain why this was such a big deal.

In previous chapters, I shared how I was one of the most sought-after marketers in Jamaica. I had been blessed not only to climb but to establish my space at the executive level in corporate Jamaica for twelve years. But suddenly, I didn't want to do marketing anymore. I had projects that I wasn't passionate about, and I became frustrated and unmotivated. I was trying to figure out what was next, and it felt like I was starting from scratch.

Financially, my savings were drained. Professionally, I was lost and felt directionless. I was grateful to be with my family and friends, but I needed to regain my drive, passion, and sense of purpose.

God truly works in mysterious ways, and His timing is always perfect. In June 2021, I attended a conference in Pittsburgh with my pastor. Even though other members of my church in Jamaica were there, this trip was really for me. By the wisdom of God, I invited my girlfriend to come with me at the last minute because I thought she needed time away, and we both needed time together. We landed in Pittsburgh and drove about twenty minutes to the hotel from the airport. That afternoon, I called my pastor to connect with him and went to a hotel two minutes from mine, which I thought was his hotel. It turned into pure comedy when I realized I had booked the wrong hotel, which was about an hour away from the conference location. Unfortunately, there was no availability at the closer hotels.

Thankfully, I had my girlfriend with me to travel the one-hour commute to and from the conference at 7 a.m. and again at 10 p.m. or midnight, depending on the day. As I sit here, writing this chapter a year later, I vividly remember how it felt to be in the presence of God at that conference, surrounded by others after not being able to attend church in person for over a year. I was able to worship freely, and I was filled—not only with the Holy Spirit but with the energy and love of those around me.

You know those moments when you try to run from God—or at least hide—because you know what He's capable of, and you're not always ready? As much as I wanted to be in His presence, I wasn't expecting any major revelations. I was praying for my girlfriend, asking God to move mightily in her life because she was in a dark place at the time, and I just wanted her to find herself again. I was in a dark place too, but in my mind, I was always functional, so I thought I was okay.

Now, let's pause for a moment. I could have easily prayed and been expectant for both of us, but I was so accustomed to being strong and in control, not dwelling in my own darkness, that it was easy to focus on someone I love instead of myself. Fortunately, the God I serve knows what I need and shows up even when I don't acknowledge that I need Him. It's okay to look out for others and show them love while also doing the same for ourselves. I'm still learning how to do that, but I'm getting better.

My journey to rediscovering who I was, and understanding that God was taking me into a new season, started at the Presence Conference in Pittsburgh, PA. Spending time with my girlfriend, Leigh, my pastor, and his family, the Morgans, was exactly what I needed.

I don't know if you've noticed, but as we say in Jamaica, "My head tough," which means I can be hardheaded. And if nothing else, God knows that about me, so He always communicates with me in a very direct way (smile). While at the conference, every day someone came and prophesied over me. They were all just confirmations of the prophecy my pastor and his mother had given me earlier that year, which I chose to ignore—not intentionally, but because I wasn't ready to receive it.

When God has a plan for our lives, the faster we embrace it, the better off we are. We can't run from it; we can only delay the inevitable. You'd think I would have learned that years ago. I'm a work in progress; God is not done with me yet (smile). Don't ever forget that we are all works in progress.

Fast forward to October 2020, when I attended another conference in Ohio with a few members from my church. I had the chance to reconnect with someone who is like a younger sister to me and to strengthen my relationship with someone who was like a big sister during my childhood. It's amazing how God places the right people in your life at just the right time. That conference wasn't an overwhelmingly spiritual experience like Pittsburgh was. Instead, it was a strategically timed opportunity with the right people, giving us the chance to support one another in the right way, at the right time, and set a foundation to build upon.

I remember that October, someone who had been a very good friend of mine for at least twelve years was going through a tough time, health-wise—both physically and mentally. Being the friend I am, I wanted to be there to support him. He had been a great support to me, and his friendship was important to me. I offered to move to the state where he was living to help him through his medical challenges. Initially, he was very receptive, but then he disappeared.

I learned a few lessons from this experience.

Lesson number one: Being supportive of a friend doesn't always look the way we expect it to. Sometimes, when people are struggling, they may choose to handle things in the way they believe is best for them. This could mean giving them the space they desire or think they need.

Lesson number two: Someone else's actions are not necessarily a reflection of me or the value I bring to a relationship. There are times when I choose to isolate myself because I need to process things in my own way and on my own time. This doesn't mean I don't love or value my friends or family. I had to remind myself that the same applies to any of my friends who may seem distant or who I feel may have shut me out.

Lesson number three, and the most valuable lesson at the time, was that good people come into our lives and add value. But sometimes, we become too comfortable, and God needs to remove those people to make room for something better—or something new—that will help us grow and thrive in a different way.

I remember going through a fast with my church at the end of October or the beginning of November 2021. I wasn't sure what I was fasting for, but I knew God was calling me to dig deeper and spend quality time with Him, so I was obedient. I gained so much clarity in areas of my life I hadn't even focused on. I became clear about two things:

The relationships I needed to release. These weren't bad relationships or friendships, but I had become too comfortable in them. God needed me to grow. Letting go of these relationships didn't mean I wouldn't speak to these individuals again or that I would stop caring about them. It simply meant I had to distance myself, step out of my comfort zone, and remain open to something new and different.

Clarity about my husband. God instructed me to write down all the qualities I believed I needed—not just wanted, but needed—in my future husband. This wasn't an easy task for me. Although I love writing lists, I rarely made lists about my personal life. I was so afraid of disappointment that I never allowed myself to truly think about the future in terms of relationships. I had experienced so many personal disappointments that I held onto my independence as long as I could. The idea of being interdependent with someone wasn't something I allowed myself to consider. When I thought about buying a house, I never thought about doing it with someone else. If I was planning for the future—insurance, wills, savings, investments—it was always just about me, my siblings, cousins, their children, and my godchildren. It never included a husband or family.

Let me remind you that I started writing this book several years ago. It has been a work in progress, and even when the publisher sent me the final edit to review, I hesitated because I knew something was missing. I knew the book wasn't complete. I felt like a hypocrite writing about self-love, self-care, embracing who you are, owning and loving yourself when, in this area of my life, I still had so many insecurities that others couldn't see, but I knew were there.

I was in a relationship for three years. Six months in, he took me ring shopping. Three years later... nothing. But God knew he wasn't the one for me. He was a wonderful man with so many great qualities. He was driven, caring, considerate, and likable. But somewhere along the way, we both realized we were prolonging the inevitable, and we made the mutual decision to separate.

I believe everyone comes into our lives for a reason, and his reason was to teach me stability, show me what it was like to be in a relationship with someone considerate and caring, and open me to the possibility of partnership and marriage.

Fast forward to late November 2022. It was Thanksgiving weekend, and I was finally in a good place again. I had done my fast, released the people God told me to let go, and was ready for something new. I was ready for whatever God had in store for me. I was approaching my 40th birthday, and I was determined to get my mind right to embrace the new professional journey God was preparing for me… or so I thought.

By now, you've probably realized that I often say we must always "live good with people." Two of my male friends, who are very dear to me, were coming to Florida for Thanksgiving and reminded me to make time for them. Without hesitation, I was excited and looking forward to their visit. They were coming for a boys' trip but still remembered to call me. It was a reminder that I am as special to them as they are to me, and that I must nurture the relationships that show they value me as much as I value them.

Who would have known that by being obedient, releasing what God told me to release, valuing the relationships that mattered, and being open to something new—even if it came in a form I wasn't used to or initially drawn to—something magical could happen? When God has a plan, nothing can stop it.

On November 28th, 2021, I met my life partner, the one God Himself chose for me. Meeting a man was the last thing on my agenda that year. As usual, I was focused on my professional development, being comfortable in my skin, and loving myself the way God wanted me to. I'm laughing as I type this because I can just imagine God laughing at me, thinking I knew exactly what I needed—or even wanted—while He was executing His perfectly orchestrated plan.

That's a story for another day, but the lessons I've learned from this encounter are:

1. Be open to doing something new: going to new places, meeting new people, and embracing new adventures.

2. Trust your circle—the people who genuinely have your best interests at heart.

3. Preparation time is important: Prepare for the opportunities God has for you so you are ready to receive them when they come.

4. Trust the process: What doesn't happen in 40 years can happen in a single day.

I was about to turn 40—forty years that felt like a desert for me—were just my preparation for the promised land. I deserve unconditional love. I deserve to be treated like a queen. I deserve to be happy. I deserve to have a partner I can grow and build with.

It is okay for me to be emotionally, financially, and professionally vulnerable with the right person. Through that vulnerability, I will learn and grow.

Growth is a constant process. It doesn't stop when we reach the "promised land." We must continue to be intentional about becoming better every day.

The right love is freeing; it brings peace, joy, and respect. It is patient and kind. It does not envy, boast, or display pride. It does not dishonor or seek its own interests. It is not easily angered and keeps no record of wrongs. Love does not delight in evil but rejoices with the truth. It always protects, trusts, hopes, and perseveres. It never fails. It honors God and remains faithful. It complements you, not completes you. It helps you grow and become better. It nurtures you and makes you feel not just safe, but truly know that you are safe.

I understand that no relationship is perfect, and all relationships—whether friendships, family connections, or marriages—require effort and good communication. They all require us to be intentional about how we nurture them. How we handle conflict matters, as does how we treat each other, even when we are not in the mood or unhappy with the other person. The same is true for how we treat ourselves, how we speak to ourselves, and how we care for ourselves—even when we are not in the mood or feel like we're in a slump. These actions will influence how long we stay in that slump or mood.

The purpose of this chapter is to remind you that growth is a daily decision. How we love ourselves and those around us is a daily choice. We never stop growing; we never stop learning. We may experience self-doubt in different areas of our lives and at various times, but we can shorten the learning curve each time. We can use different techniques to remind ourselves daily that, although we are a work in progress, we are worthy and capable of doing great things. We can remind ourselves of what we deserve in all our relationships. We can choose to do things differently at any point, regardless of our circumstances. We can choose to be ready and open to what God has in store for us, which means putting in the work and being obedient to His prompts for growth—even if it requires letting go of things or people that no longer contribute to our growth, even if they have been good to us.

My prayer is that this book has helped you, in some way, to see yourself through God's eyes, to recognize your value, and to understand who you were created to be. I encourage you to evaluate your relationships and how you are showing up for the people in your life, as well as how they are showing up for you.

Thank you, God, for the reminder that I am more than enough.

Thank you for reminding me that I am loved and I am chosen by You, and that is enough. Help me to walk in the dominion. You created me to operate in excellence, living a life of significance.

www.ingramcontent.com/pod-product-compliance
Lightning Source LLC
Chambersburg PA
CBHW071237130626
46556CB00003B/1054